MARRIAGE BY THE BOOK

THE AWESOME WORK OF ONENESS

Marilyn Fountain

New Harbor Press
RAPID CITY, SD

Fountain/New Harbor Press
1601 Mt. Rushmore Road, Ste 3288
Rapid City, SD 57701
www.NewHarborPress.com

Ordering Information:
Quantity sales. Special discounts are available on quantity purchases by corporations, associations, and others. For details, contact the "Special Sales Department" at the address above.

Marriage by the Book / Marilyn Fountain. -- 1st ed.
ISBN 978-1-63357-397-0

Contents

Acknowledgments

To my husband, Morris, the love of my life. I am grateful for the years and for the family we have built through the grace and kindness of God.

I am grateful to the women who allowed me to probe their most private moments in order to share experiences that will minister to other women about living in truth—by *The Book*.

I am grateful to my encouragers who pushed me to go beyond my comfort zone.

Preface

In the late 1970s, there was a popular television advertisement for a product called Calgon that boasted the best bubble bath beads ever conceived made of pastel granules scented with calming fragrances like lavender and rose. Its motto: "Calgon, take me away!" The idea was that by slipping into a bathtub foaming with soothing Calgon bubbles, you could get squeaky clean and, at the same time, escape to a place of utter peace and quiet. That ad sold millions of boxes of promised tranquility and, no doubt, is selling millions still.

We fall in love with expectations of a soothing experience, like a warm bath bubbling with sweet tranquility. But the kind of love required in marriage is not an escape on puffs of iridescent dreams. The peace which we achieve in marriage flows inward, deep below the epidermis, down into the soul. It is the kind of peace that comes from surrendering ourselves to the purposes of God and His plan for our marriages. We can try to get there using our own resources, whatever they may be; or we can do it by *The Book*—searching the Scriptures, spending time with Jesus in prayer and praising Him as the One Who created marriage for our good, Who has the answers to the dilemmas that challenge our marriages and Who desires to prosper us in our marriage relationships. I tried doing it my way, and I learned to do it His way, letting His nearness take me away. When I abandon myself, my emotions, and my marriage to the power of the

Lord, there is a soaking of sorts, an ineffable peace that seeps into the cracked and sore places within me and washes them with stillness. But there is always a battle before surrender. I liken it to my introduction to parasailing while vacationing in Puerto Vallarta, Mexico. There was a definite abandoning of my normal boundaries. I had to get up from the safety of my beach chair and strap myself into an apparatus that would hurl me into the sky like a human kite, flying some 500 feet above the sea on the end of a tow rope connected to a small boat. The idea of confronting gravity like that was both daunting and exciting. Emotionally, I was straining toward two opposing directions at once. I was as bold as a skydiver on the outside, scared to death on the inside. But once I let go and embraced the ride, it was as if I had become one with the air and the sounds of everything earthly were as nothing, having been sucked into the hush of the atmosphere. The stillness was profound, penetrating, and peaceful. That is what it is like for me when I surrender completely and sink into praising and worshiping the Lord. In that moment of surrender for the glory of God, everything else— my life, my emotions, and my marriage—is consumed by the silence of my soul hurling toward Jesus. It is profound, penetrating, and peaceful. I feel safe. I feel free. For me, this is reliance on God, seeking Him with all my heart, trusting Him to stay connected to me, to provide the peace I need and to help me stay above the swells that come with married life. So I trust Him with my marriage, whether I am soaking or soring. I strap myself to Him with the wisdom of the Bible and embrace His promise in Jeremiah 29:13, "You will seek me and find me when you seek me with all your heart." I have learned to take Him at His Word, trust the authenticity of Scripture, and do the awesome work of oneness, living my marriage by *The Book*.

Introduction

One Sunday morning, following our regular church service, a very godly woman for whom I have great respect approached me and prayed for me. When she finished, she looked at me very intently, almost knowingly, and told me that I should write a book about marriage. My first reaction was one of amusement at what seemed like an absurd prospect. It was a reaction much like Sarah's when the Lord told her that she would have a baby at the age of ninety. I could not imagine birthing such a vast and intimate subject. She continued to encourage me with her words of faith. I tried to push them out of my mind, convinced that I could not or, perhaps, should not tackle that subject. I had already been through one self-invasion when I had to face my personal pain following the death of my son.

Where would I begin? I am hardly a contender for the Proverbs 31 wife award. Add to that today's fluid concept of marriage compared to the day my husband and I said, "I do," and suddenly taking on that subject seemed like braving the night sea in a rubber dinghy. Nothing is as it was when I married Morris Fountain, Jr., not the frequency of marriage, the longevity of marriage, or the tradition of marriage. So I should not have been surprised when a young woman told me that she had had six partners, each of them a husband, in her view, just not in the traditional sense. Like so many in today's society, she was very much like the woman at the well, with one difference: she had not had an encounter with Jesus.

Marriage has slipped in the ratings. In 2017, the Pew Research Center released a report on US marriages, stating that in the 1960s, 72% of all adults 18 and over were married. It further showed that in 2014, only half of Americans were married, down from 57% in 2000. Even the definition of *marriage* has been challenged by the church, the state, the government, and society. More and more couples are choosing to live together rather than marry. It is a growing trend in lieu of traditional marriage. A report by the US Department of Health and Human Services articulated the shift in living styles. According to the report, "In recent years, women were increasingly likely to cohabit with a partner as a first union rather than to marry directly." Of the more than 22,000 women who were interviewed (representing various racial and ethnic groups between the ages of 25 and 44), 48% in 2006–2010 cohabited as a first union, compared with 43% in 2002 and 34% in 1995. The rise in cohabitation as a first union over this time period led to a lower percentage of women choosing to marry: 23% in 2006–2010 compared with 30% in 2002 and 39% in 1995." By age 30 the percentage of women who lived with a partner outside marriage from 2006–2010 jumped to nearly 75% compared to 62% in 1995. It seems that a large segment of American society chaffs at the idea of working through a marriage. There is no doubt that marriage can test every notion about becoming one with another person forever. Some have even called marriage the "ruination of a good relationship."

But the fact that God made marriage His first institution tells us how important it is to Him. Right off the bat He lays out His plan for marriage in the first two chapters of the Book of Genesis with the creation of Adam and Eve. They are our forebears created for marriage in oneness with the primary purpose of producing offspring to populate the earth. Although they did not repeat marriage vows, they were given to each other by God to live together for a lifetime in a covenantal union. He designed Adam to be a leader (and husband) and to work by caring for the earth and all its creatures. He designed Eve to be Adam's helpmeet (and wife) and mother of their children. God's plan was good and perfect and intended to be replicated from generation to generation. But when Eve accepted the forbidden fruit from Satan and shared it with Adam, everything changed, including marriage. Almost immediately, the formerly happy couple forgot all about their oneness. Without a second thought they began looking out for their separate interests by attempting to exonerate themselves individually, for what they had done together. In their fallen state, they made excuses for themselves, casting blame on each other and insinuation upon God rather than assuming responsibility—together. Consequences followed, bringing difficulties and disappointments. Living in oneness became less organic and more process—a process that would make choosing to love like Jesus loves (unconditionally, harmoniously, and actively) hard work. This was their legacy to every married couple to follow for all time.

Like most brides, when I married Morris I looked forward to our oneness. But I didn't realize how much work it would take to achieve it. There is no middle ground to oneness, but there is a lifetime of adjustments to make, both big and small. I am reminded of the expression: *don't sweat the small stuff.* Oddly, in marriage, often it is the small stuff that challenges us because all of us have annoying differences. Take sharing a bathroom. It is a well-known source of annoyance for many of us: He leaves hair in the bathroom sink, shower, and on the floor;

she squeezes the toothpaste tube from the middle; he leaves the toilet seat up and doesn't always flush; she uses too much toilet paper and occupies too much space with her cosmetics; he leaves the bathroom floor sopping wet after he showers; she takes forever to relinquish the bathroom. These are typical differences that have sensible solutions—or should—so that they do not become contentious. My biggest little bathroom issue was not about hair, toothpaste, or any of the like. It was about the lack of privacy. Being a newlywed, it seemed to me that there were certain things that implied way too much oneness. I was young and, except for living with roommates in a college dormitory, had lived in my parents' home up to the day of my wedding. Any personal or hygienic matters were taken care of in the context of sharing the same space with my family or other females. That was normal to me. Marriage turned all that on its head and confronted me with a completely different dynamic of normalcy and space-sharing.

Now, what I am about to say may sound ridiculous, but when I married, modesty had not yet become old-fashioned. So here it is: I didn't like using the toilet when Morris was around. (Phew! I got it out. I pray I am not the only one who has ever experienced that dread). I did not see him in the same way that I saw my parents, siblings, or college roommates. I related to him differently and wanted to be pleasing to him differently. Revealing my private habits in such a raw fashion was uncomfortable. I felt anxious and embarrassed, as if I owed him an apology for having to give in to the demands of my body. So to avoid the issue, I would wait until he left the apartment before I would allow myself to sit in peace (this was my sensible solution). I didn't mind his presence if all I had to do was to "make a river" as my mother used to say to me when I was a child. And over the course of dating, he was used to waiting while I made a quick run to the ladies' room when we were in public places. In fact (and I cannot believe I am telling this on myself), he witnessed one of my river-making moments, quite accidentally. It sounds indecent; but there is an explanation. He and I had gone on a double date with my brother and a young woman he was seeing at the time. We were driving along a busy road when my very full bladder passed the point of "soon" and progressed to the screaming pitch of "now!" The problem was that we were not near a public restroom. As we drove around a corner, I noticed a large thicket. Since it was evening, with only the moon hanging over the dark road, I decided that I could seek privacy and relief if I worked my way into the middle of the thicket where I would be hidden from view. When I returned to the car, everyone was howling with laughter. Apparently, as cars passed by my hideaway, their headlights flashed through the bushes, illuminating me in full squat making a river in the soil. It was one of my most embarrassing experiences and, at the time, not a laughing matter, at least not to me.

But, getting back to my early bride days, relieving a full bladder when Morris was around was one thing, passing the remains of my last meal was something else. I thought: what on earth would he think of me, his sweet, new bride, if he went into the bathroom after me and was met with an odious bouquet? That would be worse than the incident in the headlights! I don't remember how long it took for me to stop waiting for him to leave our apartment so that I could have a private, passing moment. For some reason, perhaps my youth, I had not imagined how all-encompassing a life of oneness would be with my husband. My view of oneness was basic: I wanted to be with him. Thankfully, that period of bathroom paranoia faded as I settled into my changed life and focused on more important and urgent adjustments.

The truth about the adjustments we must make in our marriages, whatever their nature, is that, like balloons, they can expand to become big or shrink to something small and insignificant, depending on how much air we blow into them. My fear of shaming myself before Morris simply by engaging in normal, bodily function was certainly blown out of proportion. We can inflate or deflate any situation. However, we should be careful with the big things, because they have the potential to explode. What's more, they do not come to be an annoyance to us but rather to declare war against our marriages by deploying weapons of mass destruction—things like financial meltdown, communication failure, infidelity, apathy, and worst of all, the grief of losing a child. With the exception of infidelity, Morris and I have experienced all these things and survived them by the grace of God, but at great stress to oneness. Surviving these kinds of attacks is why it is so crucial that we remember the vows we made when we were brides. Marriage is a culmination of love for God and our husbands expressed in both bitter and sweet terms, because marriage stretches us beyond our comfort zones, sometimes to the point of pain; but it is the stretching that makes us flexible and able to bend to one another; otherwise, we snap. Yet, whether our marriages are wounded or wonderful, God cares about them intensely. He knows our vows are easier said than done, "For we do not have a high priest who is unable to empathize with our weaknesses, but we have one who has been tempted in every way, just as we are—yet he did not sin." (Hebrews 4:15 NIV) He knows, too, that we need Jesus in the middle of our marriages, holding our hands, our hearts and our tongues.

So we should not forget the importance of our vows, but rather go forward in them to achieve the oneness that marriage requires, expecting the unexpected to appear—good and bad—in one form or another. We are designed to experience marriage as God intended. But for that to happen, we have to take our marriages into custody, by *The Book*, and demolish arguments and every pretension that sets itself up against the knowledge of God, taking every thought (and action) captive to the obedience of Jesus Christ, always seeking God's purpose, through oneness. (2 Corinthians 10:5) Oneness will not happen without work, sacrifice and a knowledge of God's plan for marriage; but it is where we find strength and joy and the comfort that comes from knowing that we are in God's will and, therefore, able to conquer the hard stuff when it strikes. After all, oneness is God's concept—a divine equation for carrying out His Kingdom's purpose. It is not the equation we learned in school where $1+1=2$. Marriage in God's way means $1+1=1$.

When my two daughters were planning their weddings, I told them that marriage would be the hardest work they would do, if they were to stay married. My purpose in saying that was not to discourage them. I wanted them to grasp that maintaining a marriage involves effort and care regarding the needs of both parties as well as the union as a whole. The work of marriage is a shared, self-denying endeavor by design, requiring both husbands and wives to bear weight for each other, and not only bearing weight, but persevering together through the expected and the unexpected. Difficulties will come—that's a promise. The Bible says in John 16:33, "In this world you will have trouble." Trials, troubles, difficulties, and challenges—they are one and the same, and they are as natural to marriage as a wedding band. Disagreements crop up, circumstances change, and sooner or later, anger and frustration will collide with love and happiness. What is not known is how trying the times will be or how long they will last, how frequently they will occur, or how well we will handle them and make the necessary adjustments.

I can remember the first time I felt that I was over my head, and it only took three months of marriage to get me there. At the time, I lived walking distance from my parents' home. One afternoon, I took the short trek to visit my mother and told her that I thought I had made a mistake getting married. She looked at me calmly and said, "Well, I think you will have to go home and fix your mistake." That was my first encounter with tough love, and her words were certainly tough to take—definitely not what I was hoping to hear. I don't know what I wanted to hear, but it wasn't that. Maybe I wanted a pity party or to hear her say that I could come back to her and my dad. Whatever was on her mind, it wasn't about aiding me in ditching my marriage. Had I complained of abuse of any kind, or infidelity, she would have been entirely supportive. My complaint was about differences—things that don't tend to be issues during dating or courtship when couples are together for planned periods of time and each one is trying his or her best to please the other. To me, then, marriage was like becoming a licensed driver—a coming of age, cruising through life, top down, wind in my hair, and the man I loved beside me, both of us unaffected by the noise around us or the potential for crashing into something unexpected. I was oblivious to the intricacies of married life, much less the idea that contentment and conflict could coexist in oneness.

It was a shock to my sensibilities when the unexpected came so quickly. I don't think I had ever considered the fact that, at the age of 21, I was a grown woman just like my mother, only younger and much less wise. I had not really cut the umbilical cord when I married. I simply stretched it as far as it could go. In many ways, at least in my mind, I was still the daughter of Roger and Helen Thomas. But if the totality of adulthood had eluded me, it had not my mother. By sending me back to my own home, she was teaching me that marriage is built, and it is built a little each day, like a high-rise, one story at a time, come rain or shine. I know there were times when she was completely put out by something my father did or said, but I never saw her explode out of control in anger or try to run away from home. Perhaps she unloaded her rage in private, out of earshot. What I saw in her was a strong woman who managed her home quietly with great dignity and grace. I can recall a woman saying to me when I was a teenager, "You look just like your mother. I only hope you will be as fine a person." She must have touched an exposed nerve because I still remember the irritation I felt at her comment and the sense that I was being artfully accused of falling short of my mother's measure of refinement. Perhaps she perceived that I had not inherited my mother's subtlety and poise. I came into the world prepared to speak my mind plainly—bluntly wouldn't be an exaggeration. There were many times when wisdom would have said, "Be still." It took years of practice for me to be able to resist the urge to fire off a full clip of defensive words when married life got hard. I might have saved myself a lot of angst if I had surrendered sooner to the invitation found in James 1:5, "If any of you lacks wisdom, let him ask of God, Who gives to all liberally and without reproach, and it will be given to him."

Mother was right when she told me to go home and fix my mistake. My mistake was not in getting married. It was my naïveté about what marriage would require. Premarriage jitters notwithstanding, bliss was what I had in mind when I said, "I do." I don't recall ever thinking that the differences between Morris and me mattered. In fact, at the time, I didn't think we were all that different or that he and I would have very different needs, different desires, and in some cases, different hopes and dreams.

But here's the thing: When we are standing at the altar re-splendent in our wedding gowns, even if we recognize that there are differences, we don't view them as a threat to the marriage relationship. We are at the precipice of happily- ever-after, experiencing the moment we have been waiting for with excitement and anticipation. Any differences we might have recognized are often seen as part of the attraction: charming, and if challenging: manageable. We are, after all, in love. We proclaim it amidst all the pomp and circumstance the wedding allows. We vow to stay in love, to comfort and honor our dear husbands, keeping them for better or worse, for richer or poorer, in sickness and in health, forsaking all others and being faithful only to them until death parts us. It is the most sincere, if not altruistic, commitment uttered by eager brides.

Such vows were not a factor for the world's first bride. Eve did not come to Adam in a lavish white gown on the arm of a beaming, earthly dad, proclaiming her everlasting love and devotion to him. There was no clergy to officiate nuptials, no best man or groomsmen, and no bevy of bridesmaids to celebrate the occasion. Eve was divinely created by God from and for Adam.

Why didn't God form Eve from the dust of the ground in the same way that He formed Adam? Why would He take a rib from Adam's body to fashion a wife for him instead? What was special about Adam's rib? There are 206 bones in an adult body. Why not take a bone from his spine or his feet or hands where there are 106 from which to choose? I think He chose Adam's rib because it was the bone that was closest to his heart. The ribs enclose and protect the heart, providing it a safe haven, a refuge, a hiding place, a fortress, and a shield against harm. I think God had His own character in mind when He decided to use Adam's rib to create Eve (Psalm 46:1). Adam was to be

Eve's protector, her refuge, her hiding place, her fortress, and her shield against harm in the natural world. He was supposed to guard her and love her as one who is delicate and vital to life. Eve, on the other hand, was bone of his bone, flesh of his flesh (Genesis 2:23), a perfect complement to Adam who would respect him, for without his rib, she would not have existed. But who can know the mind of God? His thoughts are higher than our thoughts; His ways higher than ours (Isaiah 55:9). However, wouldn't it be just like our omnipotent Creator to use a bone from Adam's rib, so near to his heart, to symbolize the closeness He intended for married couples to enjoy. If we are to experience this kind of closeness, we need His help.

> But how can people call for help if they don't know who to trust? And how can they know who to trust if they haven't heard of the One who can be trusted? And how can they hear if nobody tells them? And how is anyone going to tell them, unless someone is sent to do it? (Romans 10:14 MSG)

The Bible is our God-inspired messenger for truth that can be trusted. God's purpose for marriage has not changed. It is we who have changed. Our marriages are complicated by our fallen, human nature. Marriage, in the world as we know it, portends the expected and the unexpected. That is its mystique. And, in spite of arguable statistics that claim that divorce rates among Christian couples are no different than those reflected by the rest of the nation, the lure of wedding bells lives on. Bridal shops and wedding planners are plentiful and thriving as are venues of every description priced to fit any pocketbook, all to make our wedding dreams come true. The questions we must consider are these: Can we hold on to our bride-perspectives and our bride-memories when the wedding is over and we settle into being wives? Can we accept that there will always be mountains to move and storms to be still? Can we abandon ourselves to the purposes of God by doing the awesome work of oneness and living our marriages by *The Book*?

But in everyone, and of course in ourselves, there is that which requires forbearance, tolerance, forgiveness. That necessity of practicing those virtues first sets us, forces us, upon the attempt to turn— more strictly, to let God turn—our love into charity. C. S. Lewis, *The Four Loves*

Seek the Kingdom First

(Matthew 6:22)

Courtship and Dating

"His eyes are like doves by the rivers of waters,
washed with milk, and fitly set."
(Song of Solomon 5:12)

It's the oddest thing how a single trait in a person can become utterly irresistible. How many times have we heard statements like: "He's so charming," "He makes me laugh," "He has the cutest smile," "He's so intelligent," and so on.

For me, it was his eyes. I thought my husband—though he wasn't my husband at the time—had the most beautiful, penetrating eyes, as dark and mysterious as black coffee. I cannot recall the exact moment when I became enamored of them or him for that matter. Our mothers were close friends, which caused us to be around each other throughout our young lives. But I can remember being excited that I got to sit next to him in the children's Sunday school class at Holy Cross Episcopal Church in Pittsburgh, Pennsylvania. Years later, both of us were on the junior high school safety patrol team. I remember standing next to him as still as Lot's wife, strapped in my white patrol belt, more focused on the fact that he was right beside me than on listening to the duty instruction for the day; and I remember looking forward to typing class (he sat directly behind me), and sharing my Charms with him (the colorful candy squares, that is). Looking back, it was a priceless lure, which, in those days, cost a scant five-cent per pack. Maybe it was on one of those occasions. It's hard to say because I saw him regularly, not just at church and at school but on other occasions as well. By the time we were sixteen years old he had acquired a driver's license. Every now and then, he would chauffeur his mother to my house. While she visited my mother, to my delight, he visited me. We began dating in our senior year of high school. By then I was consciously aware of his lovely eyes. There were many things that I admired about him: He was handsome, polite, gentlemanly, athletic, and smart. He possessed a quiet elegance—a solidness that was gentle—that made me want to be around him. And unlike many of his contemporaries, he was not boastful. He was comfortable. I felt safe in his company. I was pretty certain that I would marry him eventually; if not him, someone with his characteristics. I never cared for the vain, life-of-the-party types or their attention-getting shenanigans. There was nothing more boring to me than a show-off or a guy who talked about himself all the time, telling me how great he was at something or other.

Back then, in my circle of friends, dating was still subject to parental approval and an understanding that it was to be above reproach. It was a time when right and wrong and acceptable and unacceptable were truths not yet muddled in a collective bent toward selfness. If we overstepped the line, we knew it. Judeo-Christian values had not quite surrendered to what would become a sweeping cultural revolution seeking self-actualization. Nor had vulgarity and immorality become a national standard for free expression. In those days, there were clear boundaries for behavior, especially in public, particularly for teenage girls and single women. I can hear my mother's voice trailing behind me every time I left the house saying, "Remember, you are a lady!" That edict contained the entire weight of conduct, trust, and consequences. It was not that her use of the term *lady* meant that she expected me to act like an adult. Rather she was reminding me that my behavior was to exemplify what was right, acceptable, modest, and proper. She was asserting her standard, which was rooted in God's standard; and it was not a subject for debate. When it came to my conduct, propriety was as essential as white gloves for Sunday church. One of my father's favorite admonitions to me was Proverbs 11: 22, "Like a gold ring in a pig's snout is a beautiful woman without discretion."

Not everyone in the Christian community approves of dating, preferring courtship for young couples instead. Typically, dating is not entered into with marriage as the end goal. Most of my dating experiences were nothing more than a casual outing with someone I liked, doing something of mutual interest. Marriage could not have been farther from my mind, although I understood that anyone I dated could become the man I would marry one day. But at that time of my life, one day was an abstract, and a distant one at that with no plausible candidates for marriage under consideration. However, there were then and still are more immediate issues regarding dating that have little to do with who might be marriage material. Casual dating can be self-centered and can run counter to good reasoning for young adults who may—and usually do—lack maturity and wisdom. In fact, dating, compared to courtship, can present greater opportunities for hurt because, unlike courtship, the purpose for being together may not be the same for both parties. With dating, there can be unspoken motives that serve the needs of one person, but not the other. I will never forget a mortifying incident I caused because I went on a date for purely selfish reasons. I was a college student at the time. There was a young man on campus who was interested in me and sought me out for conversation every time our paths crossed. His name was Lenny. He was a nice enough fellow, but not someone I had any thoughts about beyond friendship. He always made me feel that if I turned around, I would find him following behind me like a wistful puppy looking for a home. One Friday afternoon, Lenny approached me very shyly, probably expecting a polite brush-off, and asked if I would accompany him to see a film that was showing that evening. I didn't have plans, and while Lenny was not my ideal date, his offer seemed preferable to sitting in the dorm all evening. In actuality, I had hoped to see the film with a certain someone else. But I accepted Lenny's invitation on the condition that we would go to the first showing at six o'clock. I wanted to keep my options open for the eight o'clock slot, just in case. I figured that going to the early showing with Lenny would allow me the flexibility to go to the second one as well, if asked by this *someone else*. Bingo! That's exactly what happened. I thought I had set up the perfect evening for myself. All that I had to do was to make sure that I got back to the dorm in time to go out again. Lenny could not understand why I was rushing him out of the theater and across the campus. The explanation—scratch that—the excuse I gave him was feeble at best, untrue at worst. He had no idea that I was planning to thank him as quickly as possible once we reached the dorm and then wait inside for my second date to arrive. What I had not considered was that Lenny was not in a rush. As I walked out of the dorm with my second date headed for the next showing of the same film, I walked right past Lenny as he stood in front of the dorm entrance talking with some of his fraternity brothers who had come to pick up their dates. I felt lower than shoe leather and would have welcomed being swallowed up by the pavement. Not only was I caught, I had inflicted unspeakable humiliation upon Lenny as he watched me pass by with another guy right in front of his fraternity brothers who knew he had taken me to the first showing of the film. He looked utterly gobsmacked! I could hear his frat brothers laughing and taunting him saying, "Lenny, isn't that your girl?" He never spoke to me again, and I never found the courage to apologize to him. I hadn't an inkling of what in the world I could say to adequately express regret for what I had done. I think my father's words best described me on that evening. I was the pig sporting the ring in my snout. I had shown no discretion. I hurt a nice young man, took advantage of his affection for me, and lied to him. I cannot recall a time when I felt as ashamed of myself as I did on that evening. And while I can still see Lenny's stunned face, I cannot remember a thing about my second date, my highly anticipated *someone else*—not even his name. Needless to say, I never pulled a stunt like that again or used dating as a means to a selfish end.

Dating without discretion is about more than lapses into foolish self-interests. It can portend more devastating problems like abuse, date rape, or even unexpected consequences from engaging in consensual sex. This brings me to the complicated subject of sex before marriage. There are two standards: the Bible's and the world's. Thankfully, we do not stone women for engaging in premarital sex. If that were so, there would be few women alive in America. Even many Christians (who purport to believe in the authority of the Word of God) are conflicted spiritually, ethically, and emotionally when it comes to this subject. The Bible teaches that sexual intimacy is reserved for marriage. "Therefore a man shall leave his father and mother and be joined to his wife, and they shall become one flesh." (Genesis 2:24) It further admonishes against sex outside of marriage in 1 Thessalonian 4:3, "For this is the will of God, your sanctification: that you should abstain from sexual immorality." The conflict arises because God has given us free will; the fall of Adam ensures that we are tempted, and we are designed to be sexual beings. The question is how do we discipline our sexual impulses? In 2 Peter 1:5–6, we're told, "For this very reason, make every effort to add to your faith virtue; and to virtue, knowledge; and to knowledge, self-control; and to self-control, perseverance; and to perseverance, godliness." Yet it seems that secularism offers a formidable challenge to biblical teaching. Sex is marketed as an essential element for everything from blue jeans to clean hair. But despite the incessant sexualizing of society with its cavalier approach to intimacy, we should not view what the Bible calls "promiscuity" as personal liberation or feminist empowerment won from the sexual revolution. For far too many of us, it represents casualties manifested as unwanted pregnancies, STDs, abortions, HIV and AIDS, not to mention heartbreaks, some of which never heal. In a 2015 report by the Centers for Disease Control and Prevention, "Nearly half of the 20 million new STDs each year were among young people, between the ages of 15 to 24". The past fifty years have brought about a new and troubling attitude regarding the parameters of dating. You have only to turn on the television or take in a PG-13 movie to encounter this trend. Or just stand at the checkout counter of a CVS, Walgreens, or any sundries store and there will be magazines prominently placed to titillate customers with provocative images and copy for sexing up the dating experience. Well guess what? This fixation on sex is doing its intended work. For millions of women, sex and dating are synonymous and distinguished from marriage.

A conspicuous irony in this discussion is what we often refer to as the elephant in the room. In many ways, we are undermining one of the basic tenets of the women's movement intended to eradicate the perception that women are sexual objects. In a remarkable twist of direction, we are exploiting ourselves and foiling our own fight for equality of dignity by systematically objectifying ourselves. We do it with provocative clothing styled to display as much flesh as the law allows, and for what purpose? Dare I say it: to appear sexy? Restaurants (facetiously referred to as *breastaurants*) like Hooters, and Twin Peaks have no difficulty recruiting young women to don the requisite Daisy Duke shorts and peek-a-boo tops that parade their bodies before customers as if they were a menu item. Similarly, the music industry has a backlog of young hopefuls willing to articulate lewd lyrics and appear in music videos that are sensually suggestive if not obscene. Many of them profess to be Christians. Then there is internet porn—what more is there to say about that?—and the Hollywood influence, featuring women in roles graphic enough to shatter Gloria Steinem's eyeglasses, not to mention some of the red carpet attire worn by guests at the various awards events. *Sex and the Single Girl* is not just a chick-flick. It is a reality for far too many young women, many of whom profess to be Christians but are not impacted by the words in 1 Corinthians 5:11 which says, "You must not associate with anyone who claims to be a brother or sister but is sexually immoral or greedy, an idolater or slanderer, a drunkard or swindler. Do not even eat with such people." (NIV) Yet, for those who subscribe to the new morality, right and wrong are relative terms. Modesty and restraint are old-fashioned, or in more contemporary terms—old school. Yes, times are different. The taboos of the past are passé. Dating expectations are capricious, attitudes about sexuality and standards of morality are individualized. What seems to be lost in the freedom we have gained is a cultural mindset for protecting the purity of young women. Men are not under the old rules of chivalry. (When was the last time you heard that word spoken?) We are not chaperoned while in the company of men as in days past. Couples do not spend time together seated on a courting bench crafted specifically to keep them from getting too close to one another. No one wants to go back to those times. Who does not prefer freedom and choice? The challenge is not so much in how much freedom we have, but rather what we do with it, understanding the precariousness that comes with freedom, e.g., how do our sexual freedoms influence our decisions about whom we choose to marry? We may be free to express ourselves as we please and pursue romance in whatever way we choose, but to what end? At what price? The flesh is always going to seek the sexual fulfilment it desires. That is why it is called a *sex drive*. It is built in and knows one direction: onward. If not kept in check, our passions carry us away with the speed of a zip line rope, leaving us to deal with the mornings after.

Our desires are not sinful; they are natural. God has given them to us with purpose in mind and for our pleasure. But His order is not our order. His order puts consummation after the wedding ceremony, not before it. My mother would say it in a more folksy way, "You don't put the cart before the horse." Ed Young in his book *Pure* Sex writes, "Single adults who are not sexually active are subject to more ridicule and misunderstanding than those who move from partner to partner with little or no thought of permanent commitment." Even sex on the first date is not unusual: it's casual or recreational—some call it "friends with benefits." God calls it sin.

> *Flee from sexual immorality. All other sins a person commits are outside the body, but whoever sins sexually, sins against their own body.* (1 Corinthians 6:18 NIV)

One of the factors affecting the advancement of modern behavior (even among Christians) within the context of the sexual revolution is the nomenclature that establishes unmarried sex as a legitimate social and cultural norm—and a right. The language that surrounds this worldview is not burdened by warnings of consequences nor does it hold to the cautionary words found in 1 Corinthians 6:18–20: "All other sins a person commits are outside the body but whoever sins sexually, sins against their own body. Do you not know that your bodies are temples of the Holy Spirit, Who is in you, Whom you have received from God? You are not your own. You were bought at a price. Therefore honor God with your bodies." (NIV) In the language of the Bible, sex outside of marriage is sin. It is *fornication*. These words are in stark contrast to today's vernacular, which describes *unmarried sex* as lovemaking or, more casually: recreational sex, sexual freedom, sexual activity, a hookup, and other terms too vulgar to repeat. The difference in the meaning between biblical and secular terminologies both implied and inferred is vast. The short view from a mainstream perspective is that fornication is archaic; sin is relative. Lovemaking between consenting partners is good; casual sex is a prerogative. There are many women filling the pews of churches large and small who are just as accepting of and comfortable with the mainstream view. In fact, the words *fornication* and *sin* are not applicable to today's morality. I will never forget a conversation I had with a young woman who was sharing with me her desire to meet a nice single guy who had what she called "potential." At the time, she was not engaged nor was she dating anyone. During the conversation, she spoke of how much time and money she spent on her hair. When I inquired why she put so much focus on her hair (which looked healthy and well styled), she said, "I want to look as good when I wake up with him (the guy with potential) as when I went to sleep with him." She explained that she did not want her appearance in the morning to discourage him from marriage. This was a young woman who was very active in her church—an avowed Christian whose general demeanor was lovely. She did not see any inconsistency between her attitude and her Christian walk. Galatians 5:17 says, "For the flesh desires what is contrary to the Spirit, and the Spirit what is contrary to the flesh. They are in conflict with each other." In other words, we are vulnerable and fallible. We are influenced by culture and our emotions, and as we are imperfect, living in an imperfect world, we make imperfect choices sometimes that reflect our internal and external influences. We are human. We long for intimacy and a close relationship with another person, thus we are lured by romance or the illusion of romance. We lose ourselves to our passions because we need to be loved and to experience affection and the pleasures of intimacy. We confuse charm with character and exchange sex for love, comfort, loneliness, and acceptance. Or we simply fall in love and succumb to the fervor. At worst, we abandon discretion, surrender to culture, and marginalize sex as an opportunity to have a good time—no strings, no rings, just fun.

God is not ignorant of our human desires nor does He disdain us for exercising free will. After all, He gave it to us. His desire is for us to use it to do His will—to glorify Him. That is why He has provided His own *how-to* manual for managing our sexual desires. It is the Bible. In 1 Corinthians 7: 9 this is spoken of in unequivocal terms: "But if they cannot exercise self-control, they should marry. For it is better to marry than to burn with passion." Our Heavenly Father wants what is best for us. He did not send Jesus to earth to condemn us for our failings, our vulnerabilities, or our fallibilities. He sent Him to save us from them, through Him. Romans 8:1–2 assures us of that:

"Therefore there is now no condemnation for those who are in Christ Jesus. For the law of the Spirit of life in Christ Jesus has set you free from the law of sin and of death." (NIV) Neither is God shocked by our impetuosities or the dubious choices we make. He loves us with an everlasting love, imperfections and all. When we stray, we know that we can go to Him to receive His forgiveness through Jesus Christ, for it is His kindness and goodness that leads us to repentance (Romans 2:4).

Years ago, there was a laundry detergent ad that boasted: "If the whites are clean, you know the whole laundry is clean." Spiritually speaking, when God cleanses us of sin, we know that we are *holy* clean. He tells us so, saying, "I, even I, am the one who wipes out your transgressions for My own sake, and I will not remember your sins." (Isaiah 43:25 NASB) He *wipes out* our transgressions—cleans us like a powerful laundry detergent so that His Spirit can shine through us, proving that His Word is reliable. In fact, He has given us examples of His cleansing power in Genesis 38, 2 Samuel 11, and Joshua 2–6, through the lives of Tamar, Bathsheba, and Rahab—all women who engaged in illicit sex. He did not disown them; He redeemed them. He poured purpose into their lives, making them women of destiny who would bring forth the line through which our Savior, Jesus Christ, would come, their pasts unremembered, flushed from their souls like murky suds rushing down a drain. This is His testimony of compassion, of forgiveness, and of how deeply He cares for us. Jesus demonstrated that same heart when He was confronted with the adulterous woman.

> *Now early in the morning He came again into the temple, and all the people came to Him; and He sat down and taught them. Then the scribes and Pharisees brought to Him a woman caught in*

adultery. And when they had set her in the midst, they said to Him, "Teacher, this woman was caught in adultery, in the very act. Now Moses, in the law, commanded us that such should be stoned. But what do You say?" This they said, testing Him, that they might have something of which to accuse Him. But Jesus stooped down and wrote on the ground with His finger, as though He did not hear.

So when they continued asking Him, He raised Himself up and said to them, "He who is without sin among you, let him throw a stone at her first." And again He stooped down and wrote on the ground. Then those who heard it, being convicted by their conscience, went out one by one, beginning with the oldest even to the last. And Jesus was left alone, and the woman standing in the midst. When Jesus had raised Himself up and saw no one but the woman, He said to her, "Woman, where are those accusers of yours? Has no one condemned you?"

She said, "No one, Lord." And Jesus said to her, "Neither do I condemn you; go and sin no more.
(John 8:2–11)

Dating does not have to be fraught with selfishness, sexual improprieties, guilt, heart-wrenching breakups, or life-altering conditions. In its proper place, dating is an ideal way of accessing long-term relationship potential before entertaining any thoughts of marriage while, at the same time, filling our human need for companionship and closeness. Although modern culture has sullied the ideal, dating per se is not the death of moral virtue. Neither is it a promise of eventual disappointment any more than courtship is a guarantee of propriety and marriage. Millions of couples start out dating and progress to courtship, love, and marriage. In truth, either arrangement can result in moral failure if our boundaries are undefined. I can still see the soft, serious eyes of Ashley as she made that exact point without as much as a blink. She learned by shock and frightful reflection what risky business dating can be when boundaries are unclear, unestablished, or assumed.

> *I used to be so trusting. I didn't have any reservations. But I wasn't a Christian, then. One time my college suite mate and I were listening to a DJ on the radio. We thought he had this great voice, so we contacted him and invited him to go out with us. It turned out alright, he was very nice; but it was so stupid. We could have been raped!*
>
> *The thing with dating is that both people have to be on the same page from the start, then the relationship is about friendship and companionship; otherwise, it is very hard to keep the boundaries because you let your heart go ahead of you. I had so many bad experiences with guys that couldn't keep their hands to themselves. I remember meeting a guy at a club for teens. I wasn't permitted to date, but I would have him come to the house when my parents were not at home. I liked him. We had fun together.*

By her own description, Ashley was falling heart-over-head for this young man. She trusted him completely, enough to defy her parents' rules. She continued to see him after she went off to college, thinking that eventually she would marry him. Looking back, she sees a different picture. She had fallen for a guy with few or no scruples.

> *One night toward the end of my freshman year, he came to the campus to see me. We had something to drink but, very soon, I began feeling groggy. I think he put something in my drink because I fell asleep. When I woke, he was standing over me completely naked. He was about to remove my clothes when I startled him by waking up. At that time, everyone was having sex. I actually thought that if I were to have sex, it would be with him, but when he did that, it was over. That was a life-changing event and a turning point for me. I had let my guard down and it put fear in me. I knew I had to make some changes. I decided that I was going to shut down a bit—slow down on the frat parties and meeting guys. I began doing things with my girlfriends on weekends. That summer, I gave my life to the Lord.*

Advocates of courtship consider it to be a safer, more sincere relationship because it presupposes aspirations of marriage. It's not a matter of "if" a marriage will take place but "when." While courtship may not be the American norm, there are adult singles who choose courtship over dating and many parents who prefer it for their sons and daughters. More often than not, these individuals are affiliated with churches that embrace and encourage courtship. This is particularly true among evangelical congregations. Usually the pastors or appointed counselors meet with couples who have indicated a desire to court. Once the intent is confirmed, subsequent marriage counseling sessions are scheduled as couples begin an exclusive relationship centered on the details of their future life together. Barring any unexpected, deal-breaking revelation, the plans move forward. This is an exciting time for soon-to-be brides and grooms. In the Song of Solomon, we get a vivid picture of how beautiful love and courtship are supposed to be when pursued from God's point of view. Here Solomon begins to court the young Shulammite woman by speaking to her lovingly with tender words of admiration of her beauty and poise, which, to him, set her apart from all other women.

> To me, my darling, you are like
> My mare among the chariots of Pharaoh.
> Your cheeks are lovely with ornaments,
> Your neck with strings of beads. (1:9–10 NASB)

This is not an example of a man flattering a woman to gain sexual favors from her as happens with some unscrupulous men. (I mean, how many of us wouldn't just melt at being compared to the loveliness of a horse?) He is speaking from his heart, hoping to reach hers. His efforts are well-received. She is captivated by his charming manner and looks forward to his company. She watches for him and is ecstatic to see the man who is, by now, more dear than any other.

> Listen! My beloved!
> Behold, he is coming,
> Climbing on the mountains,
> Leaping on the hills!
> My beloved is like a gazelle or a young stag.
> Behold, he is standing behind our wall,

He is looking through the windows,
He is peering through the lattice. (2:8–9 NASB)

You can almost feel her heart pounding as she anticipates his nearness and observes the sinewy movement of his young frame rushing toward her. He is singularly the most handsome man alive to her, strong and agile—like a gazelle or a stag. She cannot wait to be with him, the one who adores her. Her eagerness seems to take her breath away.

Today, courtship is less poetic but no less hopeful. The search for love and marriage continues unabated, though time and culture have broadened the context. But no change is as astonishing as that which has occurred in the last twenty years with more and more courtships blossoming through social media and myriad dating sites. Online relationships are heralding a paradigm shift with regard to how singles are becoming couples. This is a growing phenomenon for both the Christian and secular communities. Everyone knows someone who met the love of her life through an electronic source, and having found him, married him! The majority of connections still occur in churches, on college campuses, in social settings, and in the workplace. However, electronic dating services, including those created for Christians, have opened a world of possibilities for single women who are not finding Mr. Right through more traditional means. The National Academy of Sciences published a study showing that more than one-third of marriages in America begin online. The study elicited data from more than 19,000 respondents who married between 2005 and 2012. The findings confirm the millions of couples who enter into dating relationships today via an electronic medium, leading to courtship and marriage. Online relationships have become the twenty-first century version of blind dating. Instead of the help of a close friend arranging an introduction to a well-regarded bachelor, an online search engine sorts through personal data and then offers up compatible prospects from which to choose and meet face-to-face. One cannot help but wonder about the safety of meeting the perfect guy who is also a perfect stranger over dinner, lunch, or a paper cup from Starbucks. Nonetheless, venturing online may not be the same as having a friend initiate an introduction, but it is undeniably the source of many successful matches and marriages. Ground rules are a must when it comes to cyber dating to ensure safety. Of course, nothing is foolproof. Many women have been hurt or killed by men whose personal profiles and presentations indicated perfect matches. That fact should put self-protection as the first order of business. A quick search of the internet will turn up a host of suggested guidelines. For example, here are ten essential rules for a first date.

Tell a friend or family member where you are going, with whom and for how long. If there is a change of plan, communicate that as well. Tell someone to text or telephone you during your meeting to see if all is well.

1. Use your own car or a taxi. Do not reveal your home address.
2. Always meet in a public place and sit where you are highly visible to others.
3. Never leave your drink or food unattended or accept a drink from your date that is not in a closed bottle. Use the ladies' room before or after your meeting.
4. Bring extra money so that you are prepared for any unexpected event.

5. Do not share personal information. If you anticipate future contact, continue communication using the dating service or establish a special email account.
6. Keep personal items in your possession at all times.
7. Have an exit plan for ending the meeting, if things are not comfortable.
8. Take mace or pepper spray with you. Of the two, pepper spray is more effective at stopping aggressive behavior.
9. Stay sober.
10. Don't let romantic notions override your common sense. Trust your instincts. If you see a red flag, take the cue.

There is a lot to consider when choosing to court or to date. This truth was given an even finer point by a discerning young woman named Roslyn who is a firm believer in the value of experience. Her experience with courtship taught her to prefer dating, even with its challenges. Thinking back to a time when her pastor disapproved of dating so strongly that he would not allow it in his church, she recalled how she followed his teachings to the letter. She said he had a motto: "If you can believe God for a car, a job, or healing, you can believe Him to bring the right person into your life."

Roslyn wrapped her dreams of finding a husband around that philosophy. She was patient and faithful to keep her heart to herself while she waited on the Lord. Several years passed before she entered into a courtship. She was certain that she had met the man who would become her husband. He embodied everything she had prayed for in a husband. He was self-assured, assertive, intelligent, and considerate. What's more, he shared her expectations about married life. He was a winner, and she had won him.

> *Matthew could be so kind. When we were courting, he was happy to do things for me. If I needed to run to the store he would say, "That's okay, I'll go." He would plan things for us to do together—he was good at arranging things. He would go all out for Valentine's Day: candy, flowers—the whole deal. He was really sweet. I was so impressed. He wasn't what you would call romantic, but because he tried so hard, it made me care for him all the more.*

But there was another side to Matthew's nature. What she saw as sweetness in him functioned tandemly with cunning.

> *He was jealous of my friends and stopped me from spending time with them. I had mixed feelings about that. Part of me didn't like it; part of me thought it was sweet that he wanted to spend that time with me. I didn't see what he was doing at first. It wasn't until later that I realized that it wasn't about spending time with me. It was about controlling me. I had accepted it because I knew he didn't have many friends of his own, and also because when you're courting, you behave in a submitted way. In your mind, you are already connected to marriage—you start to take on the attitude of a wife. Things really changed once we were married. He stopped doing the things he did to court me. He never did anything, again, on Valentine's Day.*

As time went on, more serious problems began to choke their marriage. Matthew didn't seem to like the work world and lost one job after another. Eventually, he stopped working altogether and leaned on Roslyn to carry the full financial load of running the household and providing for the two of them.

> *It was a big source of conflict in our marriage. It destroyed it. He would say that he didn't need to work anymore, that God had given me to him as a reward because he had always worked so hard. He referred to himself as the househusband. That was his excuse for staying at home while I went to work every day.*
>
> *Looking back, I can see that we didn't have friendship first. That is what was missing. Had we dated before courting, I would have gotten to know him better as a person. With courting, the emphasis in the relationship is on marriage. After going through a horrible marriage, I think dating is necessary. If we had dated before we courted, I would have seen some of his habits. We never started from ground zero. I know you never really know a person until you are married, but I think you have a better chance of seeing a bigger picture over time if you date as friends first.*

At the crux of all this discussion about dating versus courtship is this: There is risk in relationships; the closer the relationship, the greater the risk. Every time we enter into a relationship with another person we run the risk of being vulnerable. Marriage is no exception. We become expectant, which exposes our desires and needs and how much we are willing to invest of ourselves for the benefit of the relationship. If the relationship proves to be unworthy of our investment, we suffer. Sometimes that suffering turns to fear. There is an old adage that says, "Once burned, twice shy." In terms of dating and courtship, it means that when we are wounded by the relationship, often we are afraid to invest in another one in the same way. The problem with locking the door to our hearts because we are afraid of being hurt is that we risk becoming hardened and captive to an unholy spirit. This spirit has one purpose in mind: to kill, steal, and destroy our ability to experience the joy of loving and being loved as God, Who is love, intended when He said, "Let us make man in Our image, according to Our likeness" (Genesis 1:26). The Bible tells us in 2 Timothy 1:7 that God did not give us a spirit of fear. He gave us power, love, and a sound mind. Through Him Who loves us, we have these things, and with the wisdom of experience, we are able to let go of our hurts and fears and make better decisions about how and with whom we invest our time, our hearts, our trust, and, ultimately, our lives.

Working Out Oneness

Think back to your dating and courting days. What was the one feature that impressed you most about the man? How important is that feature to you today?

_____

If you could start all over again, would you date or court? Why?

_____

Would you say you were naïve or wise in managing your dating relationships?

_____

Did you ever feel unsafe or manipulated by someone you dated? How did that experience affect you?

_____

Have you ever been a Proverbs 11:22 woman? How?

_____

What has God done to open your eyes to something in your character that you need to change? How has that revelation re-shaped your attitudes and behaviors today?

How would you classify your dating/courtship memories: wonderful, exciting, happy, difficult, painful, disappointing, regrettable, or any of the above? Explain.

Do you believe you had the appropriate boundaries in place when dating or courting? How do your dating relationships intersect with your concept of a marriage relationship?

Do you feel that the values of the culture have compromised your own values? If so, how?

The debate about dating versus courtship is largely about preserving the purity and integrity of the relationship. How did your choice create a foundation for marriage?

_____

What does 1 Corinthians 6:18 mean to you?

_____

Have you ever opened your heart too much or too soon to someone and been hurt as a result?

_____

What wonders did God work in your heart that brought healing to your pain from disappointments during your time of dating or courting? How important is that healing to a marriage relationship?

_____

If Solomon were alive today, pursuing you, do you think you would be receptive to his advances? Why, or why not?

_____

Marry Me

May your fountain be blessed, and may you rejoice
in the wife of your youth.
(Proverbs 5:18)

If words were jewels the atmosphere would be ablaze with sparkles whenever Megan speaks. Her joyful spirit is buoyant—almost palpable; and when she recalls the evening of her engagement, her deeply dimpled cheeks bracket her smile like parentheses enclosing a glorious moment in time. Every detail is as vivid in her mind as when it happened, when Eric surprised her and asked the long-awaited question in the presence of friends, and with the poeticism one would expect to see in a scene from a romantic movie: "Will you marry me?" he said. In an instant, engagement to Eric, once a secret in her heart, was suddenly a tangible, dazzling reality poised on her finger, like a brilliant star filled with her every wish and the promise of love for the rest of her life.

> *We went to a restaurant for appetizers with a group of friends, in downtown Houston. Actually, I was anticipating our engagement. So I asked Eric which romper he thought I should wear, the black one or the white one? He said, "Wear the black one." I thought, "It's not happening tonight." But he was agitated, and he kept rushing me, so I thought,*

47

"Maybe he's trying to surprise me." I decided that I would wear the white one, just in case.

We got to the restaurant. We were sitting around talking, and Eric's buddy said, "Megan, that's the building where I work," pointing to the Chase Tower. I knew that Eric and his buddy had already gone to the lounge on the rooftop of the Tower about a month earlier. I didn't know that the plan was to get me up there for the proposal. I said, "I am so jealous that you and Eric have already gone to the rooftop, I really wanted to go there." Eric said, "Oh, you want to go? Let's go right now." When we got to the rooftop, I was thinking, "This would be the perfect place for a proposal." We walked to a corner where the sunset was happening. Eric asked a waitress if she would take photos of us. As she began taking the photos, Eric went up to her and repositioned the camera. When he turned around, he was holding the ring and a Bible. I realized what was about to happen. He read three Scriptures to me. The last one was Proverbs 18:22, "He who finds a wife finds a good thing, and obtains favor from the LORD." He said, "I love you, and I want you to be my wife for the rest of my life. I want to forever find favor with you in the LORD." It was so sweet. I cried as he put the ring on my finger.

Men have been popping the question in one form or another since God said, "It is not good that man should be alone; I will make him a helper comparable to him" and Adam responded by saying, "This is now bone of my bones and flesh of my flesh;

she shall be called Woman, because she was taken out of Man."
(Genesis 2:8, 23)

Probably no phrase in all the languages of mankind carries more potential for redefining a woman's position in society and culture than the words: *Marry me.* They imply a lifelong commitment not just to a husband but to oneness that supersedes all other relationships. Like Velcro fibers that fasten one fabric to another, these words are intended to convey the binding together of two lives in an interlocking way. These are daring words. Sometimes, they stumble out in sheer fright and excitement; other times, they erupt spontaneously like a loud thump from a lovestruck heart; while at other times, they struggle to get out because there is history tugging at them—eyewitness accounts of other people's marriages: their parents, relatives, and friends. Any way you look at it, a proposal of marriage is a serious and wonderful expression of love laid bare, if not courageous.

One of the most touching declarations of love for a prospective bride I have come across was to my aunt many years ago by her enraptured fiancé. Much like the lover in the Song of Solomon, he could barely contain his desire to be with her, so he poured out his adoration in a two-page letter, handwritten in cursive strokes that rose and fell like notes on a music staff. I discovered the letter following her death. It was in an old department store gift box, which, though yellow with age, still had its original satiny finish. Yet, inside, scattered among clippings, notifications, and old photos were letters in small envelopes—perfectly preserved paper time capsules, each one holding the secret things of her heart. One of the letters read as follows:

Hello My Darling,

Thanks for a wonderful evening and the (birthday) cake. I love you so much, and your kindness and thoughtfulness made me happier than I thought I would ever be. I know that we have had some rough times, but I would gladly start from the beginning because I know that one day, you will be all mine to love and to cherish—and yes, even obey, for I would like to do all things that would make you happy.

I hated to see you leave. When I put you on the train, I felt like a little boy who was losing his mother. And you looked so lovely in your black suit and the hat you so seldom wear. And you know what, since we've known each other, it's the first time I haven't seen you in 48 hours. I think it's grand to be in love, and in love with someone like you. You are everything to me. No softer lips will I ever know and no other will I ever hold in my arms. You know what, I hope that when we are married and blessed with children, and if they are all girls, they will be like you: kind, thoughtful, and so sweet.

Goodnight, darling. If I could come into your dreams I would, so that I could share them with you, too. Thanks, again, and with all my heart, truly, I love you.

P.S. I hope the next time we blow out candles it will be for you, and in our home.

Not every engagement is the culmination of what we in Western culture think of as two people in love. In many nations around the world, engagements or betrothals are arranged by parents seeking an advantageous union for their children. This type of matchmaking is as old as mankind, and while it may be obligatory, it is not necessarily objectionable or devoid of romantic love. In 1 Samuel 18:20, we see that King Saul's daughter, Michal, is very much in love with David even before she is promised to him. Her story of love reads like a page torn from a book of fairy tales. We could call it *The Princess and the Poor Shepherd Boy*. In storybook style, we see the daughter of a king pining away for a man of lowly station—a sheepherder whom her father hates. But in her eyes, David is a hero, a valiant warrior, and a gifted musician. In fact, it is his skill on the harp that proves to be the medicine King Saul needs to subdue his deranged mind and psychotic outbursts. As the story unfolds, we see that Michal is completely enamored of David. When King Saul becomes aware of her feelings, he connives to use them as a means to destroy David. He sends word to David offering Michal's hand in marriage and the venerable position of son-in-law to the king. But there is a condition. David must pursue the Philistines, Saul's archenemies, kill them and exact 100 foreskins from the slain soldiers and bring them to him. In Old Testament times, this could be considered David's *mohar* or bride-price (usually paid to the bride's father by the groom's father). In the traditional Hebrew context, the *mohar* is a monetary gift or something valuable and precious given and received in honor of the proposed union. In this case, the bride-price is a pound of Philistine flesh—a dishonorable, gruesome requirement by a neurotic, dissipating king. Michal has no idea that her father is using her as bait to force David into a dangerous and, potentially, deadly situation. All she knows is that

David is willing to accept her father's outrageous terms to earn her hand. Saul's behavior is irrational to say the least. David is hailed by all of Israel for his fighting prowess in routing the Philistines. The women of Israel have praised him singing, "Saul has slain his thousands, and David his tens of thousands" (1 Samuel 18:7). Moreover, he has fought and killed a bear, a lion, and, miraculously, Goliath, with nothing more than a sling and a stone. What are 100 Philistine foreskins to him? David is undaunted by his assignment. He is brave, ambitious, and secure in his faith in God. Romans 8:31 says, "If God is for us, who can be against us?" To His glory, David returns safely, not with 100 Philistine foreskins but 200, winning the right of betrothal to Michal.

> Many are the plans in a person's heart,
> but it is the LORD's purpose that prevails
> (Proverbs 19:21)

Although engagements among Christians are pretty straightforward and devoid of outrageous feats of courage as a brideprice, there are protocols that run the gamut when it comes to how and to what extent parents will be involved. One can only imagine the anxiety Eric felt as he planned his conversation with Megan's father. What would he say? How would he say it? And how would he show proper deference to the man who has loved Megan with a depth that only a doting father can fathom? It was a conversation that could not be avoided. Megan had a plan of her own to ensure that Eric would be well received.

> I was raised to understand that when you date, you date to marry. The thing that my dad wanted to see in Eric was his spiritual development. He believes

that everything follows that. In other words, a man who is spiritually developed will be faithful, and a good head of household. Of course, there are lots of things that he appreciated about Eric, like good manners and a good work ethic. But I knew what mattered most to him. I wanted him to see by my actions that Eric was the right person and the one I wanted to be with. So I just kept bringing him around. I didn't want either of my parents to have a reason to say no to us. They saw that he was coming to church, regularly, and to the house. They got to know him. When Eric talked with my dad about wanting to marry me, he got his blessing.

Like a modern-day Shulammite, Megan adored Eric. He was her beloved and she was his. But it took time and being with him to eventuate into courtship, love, and a commitment of marriage. Their love styles were different. Eric's was tentative and measured like a surfer assessing a swell. Megan's, on the other hand, was effervescent. She dove into the deep fearlessly, freely, like a child jumping into a rushing wave.

We met online. I knew after three months that I wanted to marry him. We talked for a couple of weeks before meeting for the first time, at Starbucks. We were attracted to each other because of our faith. Pursuing God was a focal point for us; we had the same values. He knew what he wanted in life, and he was interested in my life goals. When I told him that I wanted to be a great wife and mother one day, and a support in my community, he was fine with that. I loved that about him. I

loved a lot of things about him. He was his own per-
son—level-headed, not rash. He processed things. I
also loved the way his eyes would squint up when he
smiled. Perfect!

Wait for the LORD;
Be strong and let your heart take courage;
Yes, wait for the LORD.
(Psalm 27:14 NASB)

Although Megan felt certain that Eric was the one for her, she prayed about their relationship and sought the Lord for His will in their lives. Those early months of dating and praying brought a deepening sense of peace to her heart and mind, and a comfortable kinship with Eric. In his book *The 5 Love Languages*, Gary Chapman quotes psychiatrist M. Scott Peck saying, "If we have any purpose in mind when we fall in love it is to terminate our own loneliness and perhaps ensure this result in marriage." He goes on to say that "the in-love experience does not focus on our own growth or on the growth and development of the other person. Rather, it gives us the sense that we have arrived and that we do not need further growth. We are at the apex of life's happiness, and our only desire is to stay there."

But Megan was more pragmatic than that. She was interested in Eric's growth and development as a person and husband just as she was interested in growing and developing her own ways, within the context of their love relationship. She had no illusions about the challenges that love and living in oneness with a husband present. She was clearheaded about the unromantic things that can gnaw at a marriage—things like differences, emotions, and attitudes—issues that become little foxes eating at the foundation of marriage if they are not well-managed.

Counseling was a great help. We were both vola-
tile when we fought about things. We learned to
communicate better, to listen and not snap, to step
back, think things through, and apologize to each
other. We learned to mirror Christ's love and bring
Him out in the way that we behaved.

Indeed, Christ-likeness should be the cornerstone in a Christian marriage and not something that is dressed up for the wedding only to be left on the church steps once the ceremony is concluded. Scripture is clear regarding God's perspective on what is most important: "Seek first [Be concerned above all else with] God's kingdom and what God wants [his righteousness]. Then all your other needs will be met as well [these things will be given to you]" (Matthew 6:33 EXB). Understanding headship is equally important in a marriage. In 1 Corinthians 11:3, we are reminded "that the head of every man is Christ, the head of woman is man, and the head of Christ is God." God has called husbands to carry the mantle of leader in the home. However, if they do not or will not lead, guess what? We wives do it for them. There's an amusing example of how far misplaced leadership can go.

A man died and went to heaven to find two signs
above two different lines. One sign said: "All those
men who have been dominated by their wives,
stand here." That line of men seemed to stretch off
through the clouds into infinity.

The second sign read: "All those who have nev-
er been dominated by their wives, stand here."
Underneath the sign stood one man.

He went over to the man, grabbed his arm and said, "What's the secret, how did you do it? That other line has millions of men and you are the only one standing in this line."

The man looked around with a puzzled expression and said, "Why, I am not sure I know. My wife just told me to stand here."

Humor is a wonderful thing. It can hit us in our funny bone with hard truths, which delivered otherwise, would smart. The Bible is our source for God's divine truth and order established before the creation of the world and mankind. The collapse of the Garden of Eden is a perfect example of why God's order is the best order. He appointed headship over the affairs of Eden and Eve to Adam. When Adam failed to uphold his responsibility, Eve stepped into his role and out of God's order. The fallout was disastrous. A husband's call to headship is an imperative for him to bring order, responsibility, and stability into the home. That said, it is not meant to be a monolithic decree that cannot bend to his wife's strengths or recognize that there are times when she can and should prevail. Rather it should be viewed as an aspect of balance, of love and mutual respect, not justification for a dictatorship. The Bible illustrates a clear example of a wife exercising leadership qualities. In the story of Priscilla and Aquila, we see that it is she who is mentioned first in most verses. She was an equal partner with Aquila in their family business and in establishing a home-based church (Acts 18:3 and 1 Corinthians 16:19). And it was she who was more prominent in the teachings of Jesus Christ. Her leadership was not an overreach. It was accepted by Aquila and honoring to him because of their mutual respect and the fact that they were in one accord. However, it is patently inappropriate for a wife to usurp her husband's role and undermine his position as head of household. Likewise, it is just as inappropriate for a husband to abandon his responsibilities out of laziness, including his role as spiritual leader, and be content to let his wife carry the weight.

Sadly, for many husbands—even churchgoing believers who claim Jesus Christ—the concept of leading in their marriages is vague at best, particularly in the area of spiritual leadership. The importance of spiritual leadership in a marriage cannot be overstated. It is known by many names: the glue, the foundation, the core, the heart, and so on. These characterizations are synonymous in that each alludes to strength and stability without which Christian couples will struggle. Over time, their marriages will weaken and, as so often happens, fall apart. They become like the house built on sand that Jesus talked about in Matthew 7:24–27, "And the rain descended, the floods came, and the winds blew and beat on that house, and it fell. And great was its fall."

The period of engagement is an ideal time to talk about building a marriage by *The Book*, establishing leadership in general and spiritual leadership in particular. In fact, nothing is more important than setting the criteria for how God's order will manifest within the complexities of married life. Thus, the period of engagement should be a time of preparation—of building a house on a strong foundation, one that will not scorch under the blazing heat of life's stresses or crash when the storms come. But as crucial as leadership concerns are when planning a shared life, they should not become spoilers because of differing opinions as to how they should be carried out. They must be expressed with understanding and appreciation of one another's views, so that the beauty of this special time is not undermined! The period of engagement should sparkle with joy like the diamond by which it is represented. It should shine with love, happiness, and faith in God.

Working Out Oneness

What is the most memorable moment of your engagement?

_____

What would you say is the purpose for a time of engagement? Was your purpose satisfied? In what way?

_____

How often do you reflect on your time of engagement? What feelings are evoked in you when you remember?

_____

How important was the support of your parents when you decided to marry?

_____

Would you say that you had the heart of the Shulammite toward your fiancé?

_____

Do you fall in love easily? Are you the giver or taker in the relationship?

What do you look for in a husband?

Did you and your fiancé have marriage counseling? If so, has it made a positive difference in your marriage?

What are your expectations of your husband as a spiritual leader? Do they coincide with God's view, and in what ways?

How strong is the foundation that supports your relationship? How does Matthew 7:24–27 intersect with your thinking about marriage?

What does unequally yoked mean to you?

_____

Did you ever have second thoughts about getting married? If so, why?

_____

When you reflect on your engagement, would you say that you and your fiancé had the same life goals?

_____

Here Comes the Bride

She walks in beauty, like the night
Of cloudless climes and starry skies;
And all that's best of dark and bright
Meet in her aspect and her eyes....
Lord Byron, "She Walks in Beauty"

I have no idea why I selected the violin, but when Mr. Lewis instructed the class to pick an instrument, that is what I chose. That was a long time ago. I was in elementary school, about to have my first music lesson. I liked the way the violin felt sitting snugly under my small chin as if it were an extension of me. Maybe that was the fascination. I practiced daily, sawing away with my rosin-coated bow. How my parents stood the horrors that reverberated through the house as I forced my will upon the agonized strings I will never understand, except that parents know how to suffer lovingly when their child is tackling a challenge: they grin and bear it, ever the encouragers. The fact that my renditions of "Baa, Baa, Black Sheep" and "Mary Had a Little Lamb" sounded like the squeals from a terrified animal succumbing to a merciless predator was insignificant compared to my budding cultural development.

One of the great perks of being in Mr. Lewis's music class was the midsemester field trip to hear the Pittsburgh Symphony Orchestra perform. It was on such a trip that I heard Mendelssohn's "Wedding March" played so exquisitely it sounded like the notes were falling from heaven. It was the most thrilling experience. When my father came home from work that evening, I said, "Daddy, I want the Pittsburgh Symphony to play at my wedding!"

That was my second wedding fantasy. The first one (the one that created a permanent file in my memory) occurred at the wedding ceremony of Eva and James Hoggard. I was six years old and completely awestruck by the grandeur of the occasion as I watched with my family. The bride seemed to glide down the aisle, almost fairylike, her white gown floating softly behind her. The groom was tall and handsome, by little girl standards. When he repeated his vows, his deep, baritone voice echoed through the sanctuary like the triumphant boom of a kettle-drum. I did not know then what a serious matter those vows were to the two of them. All I knew was that I wanted to get married one day in a dress like hers to someone who sounded exactly like him. How many of us have walked down the aisle intoxicated by the aesthetics and our dreams of oneness without a realistic understanding of the covenant of marriage, its true purpose or its Creator? Proverbs 3:13–15 reminds us that, "Blessed are those who find wisdom, those who gain understanding, for she is more profitable than silver and yields better returns than gold. She is more precious than rubies; nothing you desire can compare with her."

These are the words of King Solomon originally intended for his son. God had given Solomon "wisdom and very great insight, and a breadth of understanding as measureless as the sand on the seashore." (1 Kings 4:29 NIV) No one could have offered better counsel than this man whom God had honored with knowledge greater than any man before or after him. No one was more qualified to give good counsel on matters of life, living, and choices. Solomon went on to say in verses 21–23, "Do not let wisdom and understanding out of your sight, preserve sound judgment and discretion; they will be life for you, an ornament to grace your neck. Then you will go on your way in safety, and your foot will not stumble." It is interesting that Solomon's sage advice did not carry over to his own life, especially with respect to his many marriages. He had 700 wives of royal birth and 300 concubines. In an era when polygamy was common, he had to be the champion polygamist of all time. Scripture says that "he held fast to them in love."

It seems to me that Solomon was in love with love. Like a child in awe of a glorious wedding, he wanted what he saw. He became infected with notions of romance and sensuality as his emotions pushed him, seemingly incessantly, toward the women he desired. In the end, it cost him his kingdom and stature (1 Kings 11:9–13), and his greatest gift: his wisdom. All that was left of his empire was one tribe, which God allowed him to keep, to bequeath to his son. It was a divine gesture of grace from God to honor His promise to King David, Solomon's father: "Your house and your kingdom will endure forever before Me; your throne will be established forever." (2 Samuel 7:16)

King Solomon's many weddings were no doubt occasioned by unimaginable majesty and splendor. But the true concept of marriage must have escaped him entirely. A wedding is not a marriage. A wedding is done in a day. Marriage is done every day. A wedding does not shape character, but marriage can. In its proper form, marriage is like a flowerpot for containing, growing, and displaying the lovely things of God in us. When well-potted, two lives intertwine and bloom in separate ways, yet, in one accord. This was God's plan from the beginning. He saw that it was not good for man to be alone, "So the LORD God caused a deep sleep to fall upon the man, and he slept; then

He took one of his ribs and closed up the flesh at that place. The LORD God fashioned into a woman the rib which He had taken from the man, and brought her to the man. For this reason a man shall leave his father and his mother, and be joined to his wife; and they shall become one flesh." (Genesis 2:21–22, 24 NASB) In Ecclesiastes 4:9–12, the Lord further states that, "Two are better than one, because they have a good reward for their labor. For if they fall, one will lift up his companion. But woe to him who is alone when he falls, for he has no one to help him up. Again, if two lie down together, they will keep warm; but how can one be warm alone? Though one may be overpowered by another, two can withstand him. And a threefold cord is not quickly broken."

Needless to say, my wedding day did not resemble the imaginings of a six-year-old little girl nor did the Pittsburgh Symphony show up to announce my arrival with a breathtaking performance of Mendelssohn's "Wedding March." My wedding gown was not like the one worn by Eva Stanton so many years before, and my groom did not have a voice that boomed through the sanctuary like a kettledrum. I walked toward my future and the man who would be my husband, hanging on my father's arm for the last time, in the church that had been my family's spiritual home for three generations. It was a surreal walk to a sonorous tune that echoed from the pipes of the grand organ and filled the Gothic atmosphere with the only music allowed by Father Parker. I was passing from one world to another and between the two men I dearly loved: the one who gave me life and the one with whom I would live my life. Behind me flowed a billow of white silk organza edged with pearls and stitched in place by my mother's hands. The walk to join my handsome husband-to-be seemed miles long. Emotionally, I was whirling amidst a flurry of "Oh, my gosh" thoughts. I was nervous, happy, excited, anxious, and gloriously frightened. I was fully aware that I was about to entrust the rest of my life to another. I had no idea what it would be like to live out that kind of togetherness on a daily basis. But every step I took was a leap of faith and a declaration of my love.

Not only that, it was a culmination of many talks Morris and I had about marriage, most of which were built on the assumption that, of course, we would marry. Then one day, he proposed to me officially in a letter. We were college students at the time, attending different schools, 250 miles apart. Morris hated the distance between us and complained about it in every letter he wrote to me. It was in this context that his proposal came, ardently penned on the last page of what was, otherwise, a typical letter from him. This is what he said to me:

> *I know that only when you get married can you find true togetherness. The reason is that individual freedom is, in a way, given up and the two become one: togetherness. I guess then, that ours isn't a complete love until marriage.*
>
> *Marilyn, will you please marry me? As long as you are free, I only live for you. I know I don't have much to offer now except me, and I'm not sure if I am really much. I'm worth a couple thousand dollars in insurance when I die. We won't be able to get married for a couple of years, so, although I really mean the proposal... I better take a rain check for about two years.*

He signed it, *I love you, Morris*. We were married three years later in the church of our youth, where he was an altar boy and where I sang in the junior choir.

Few ceremonies rival a wedding in planning and pageantry. According to an article published in *The Wedding Report, Inc.*, the average cost of a wedding is $26,720, not including the honeymoon, and is considered a reasonable baseline figure. Other estimates are as high as $35,329, with some East Coast cities averaging $80,000. Though many couples spend less than $10,000, there are a variety of variables that influence the overall cost up or down, including region, season, style, and even a particular day of the week, making a wedding, at any cost, a big-ticket item.

The wedding industry is a multibillion-dollar enterprise able to fulfill every bride's dream for her big day. And, indeed, it is a big day. But a wedding, however magnificent, does not make a good wife any more than a graduation ensures success in a career. A bride is a bride for a moment; a wife is a wife for a lifetime. It is important that we remember the time when we were brides, when everything was splendid and the very sight of the men we were about to marry brought utter joy to our hearts. We saw no imperfection in them as they stood waiting at the altar, watching with wonder glistening in their eyes because we were drawing nearer to them, soon to be one with them. Any flaws they may have had were veiled by the boundless love we had for them.

Why am I harping on this? It's not for reasons of romance or nostalgia. It is because of the days when we no longer look at our husbands through the eyes of a bride—the days when our love is sorely tested and tried by angry words, unexpected circumstances, disappointments, frustrations, betrayals, too much or too little of anything or everything. That's why we need to remember. We need to remember that our husbands were not perfect when we married them even if we could see no imperfection then; and they will never be perfect. More important, they are not carbon copies of us in a different skin. They are who God created them to be: different from us. If they thought exactly like us, acted exactly like us, and responded exactly like us, they would not add anything to us. We have all heard it said, "He completes me." In fact, that is God's purpose and design for marriage, but not as the singular role for our husbands. We, as wives, are supposed to complete them as well. That is how we actualize oneness. This is not a challenging concept for brides. It is challenging only after we are wives faced with the conflicts and stresses that arise when two people are a collective body of one, confronting circumstances that rail against unity. Such conflicts and stresses come as enemy forces ready to do battle, to wear us down, poison our thoughts about marriage and, eventually, our marriage relationships. When this happens, love loses its luster. We forget why we fell in love with our husbands, why we strolled down the aisle eager to say our "I dos," and why we are made complete by their presence and position in our lives. Think about Job's wife. She experienced more conflict and stress in her marriage than anyone, certainly anyone I can recall. In Job 1:13–22, we find Job's sons and daughters gathered around a dinner table fellowshipping and enjoying a meal together. Job and his wife (whose name is never given) were going about their daily affairs. They had a good life in the land of Uz. They were prosperous and respected. In fact, they were the wealthiest couple in the east. Their children were successful, and by all appearances their marriage was strong. Then, out of the blue, the unexpected happened. Satan targeted Job and carried out a vicious assault against him and his entire family.

Now there was a day when his sons and daughters were eating and drinking wine in their oldest brother's house; and a messenger came to Job and said, "The oxen were plowing and the donkeys feeding beside them, when the Sabeans raided them and took them away—indeed they have killed the servants with the edge of the sword; and I alone have escaped to tell you!"

While he was still speaking, another also came and said, "The fire of God fell from heaven and burned up the sheep and the servants, and consumed them; and I alone have escaped to tell you!"

While he was still speaking, another also came and said, "The Chaldeans formed three bands, raided the camels and took them away, yes, and killed the servants with the edge of the sword; and I alone have escaped to tell you!"

While he was still speaking, another also came and said, "Your sons and daughters were eating and drinking wine in their oldest brother's house, and suddenly a great wind came from across the wilderness and struck the four corners of the house, and it fell on the young people, and they are dead; and I alone have escaped to tell you!" (Job 1:13–19)

Where was Job's wife when this terrible news was being delivered? My guess is that she was right beside him listening to every horrifying report. The sheer repetition of bad news must have seemed apocalyptic to both of them. They had lost their children, their servants, their livestock, and the financial secu-rity they had enjoyed. In one fell swoop everything was gone. She and Job were shattered by the succession of catastrophes that took all but their lives. Nonetheless, Job responded in a way that honored God.

> *Then Job arose, tore his robe, and shaved his head;*
> *and he fell to the ground and worshiped. And he said:*
> *"Naked I came from my mother's womb, and naked*
> *shall I return there. The LORD gave, and the LORD*
> *has taken away. Blessed be the name of the LORD."*
> *In all this Job did not sin nor charge God with*
> *wrong. (Job 1:20–22)*

But there was more to come. Satan struck Job with boils that covered him from the top of his head to the soles of his feet. So horrible were the boils that he would scrape them with a piece of broken clay just to get relief. (Job 2:7–8) It had to be an unimaginable misery made worse by all the losses. Though the focus of the story of Job is on him, surely his wife was be-sieged by profound grief. Her entire existence had become a wasteland. In her distress, she became embittered and forgot to love God Who was her ultimate provider—the One Who gave her husband the ability to gain wealth. (Deuteronomy 8:18) It was God who opened her womb and allowed life to form and develop into the children she bore. It was God Who loved her first, before she ever knew Job's love. In forgetting God's love, she ceased being loving. In this darkened state, she said the un-thinkable to her poor, tormented husband: "Do you still hold fast to your integrity? Curse God and die!"

At the time of Job's test, I am sure he did not resemble the man who was once an eager groom with a bright future before him. And I am just as certain that his wife did not look like the adoring bride she was once, who saw no imperfection in her beloved husband-to-be. Conflict and stress in a marriage have a way of blurring our vision, exposing our least attractive qualities. What Job and his wife went through would test the character and resolve of any couple and demolish most marriages. How many of us fail to restrain ourselves when our own circumstances are painfully stressful and we feel helpless to change them? How many of us speak words that should never be in our thoughts and hurl them at our husbands because we are angry and have lost control or are simply exhausted from the pressures of unresolved issues? And what about the times when stress on the home front is so all-consuming that there is no mutuality— no oneness—and our deepest needs are not being met? Kathy Collard Miller and D. Larry Miller write in their book *What's in the Bible for Couples*, "Only God is capable of meeting our needs completely. Although He often provides love and joy through another person, no one except God is selfless enough to want the very best for us all the time. When we take our eyes off our spouse as the one responsible for our happiness and look to God instead, we will experience the best kind of satisfaction."

Go back with me to Job's wife for a moment. There is a spiritual aspect to her relationship with Job that has everything to do with her emotional outburst of bitter words and it is this: at the very second when she transitioned from being a bride to being Job's wife, she became one with him. The Bible establishes this fact in both the Old Testament and the New Testament. "But from the beginning of the creation, God made them male and female. `For this reason a man shall leave his father and mother and be joined to his wife, and the two shall become one flesh'; so then they are no longer two, but one flesh." (Genesis

2:24 and Mark 10:6–8) Because they were one flesh, everything that affected Job affected her. When Job prospered, she prospered. When Job was attacked by Satan, she was attacked by Satan. When Job suffered, she suffered. When he was helpless, she felt helpless. Everything that he lost, she lost as well. Thus, though her comment to him was vile, inexcusable, and completely unsympathetic to his condition, she spoke out of their oneness manifested as mutual suffering. We don't know if she regretted her words; the Bible doesn't offer insight in that regard. What we know is that God, in His infinite mercy, restored everything that was taken twofold, and blessed them with ten more children: seven sons and three daughters.

It is amazing that their marriage withstood the force of such a wild storm. They experienced the worst of each other, and even though God restored everything that was taken from them, it's hard to believe that the terror of what they endured did not burrow into the deepest parts of their souls. It is one thing to restore material wealth; it is another thing to restore ten lost children. I imagine that if we could look into their hearts we would see that there are hollows left behind—places where grief flowed like the erosive waters that carve canyons—constantly—silently, for the ten who died. Yet, in spite of their catastrophic losses and the tensions that arose between them, they pressed on together, in oneness, no longer considering the things of old, but walking in the new thing that God was doing in their lives, and in the joy of the Lord.

I think it is safe to say that Job's wife is not a poster girl for wives. But her story offers a lesson in how important it is to remember the time when we were brides, when our faces glowed with happiness because we anticipated the happiness to come; when we were dazzling in our wedding gowns that, by their sheer luxury, signified the ardency of the moment. We need to think back to the moment when our heart's desire was to be one with the men we loved, and oneness was the epitome of a perfectly shared life with them. We should press those fragrant memories into the pages of our minds and never forget the day that we made a covenant with God and our grooms—in the presence of God and a sanctuary filled with family and friends—to uphold our marriages for the rest of our lives, come what may, because we were no longer two, but one flesh.

But let's be frank. Maintaining a bride-perspective for the rest of our lives is not easy. In fact, sometimes, it's not wanted. Sometimes, all we want is a crawl space to curl up in where we don't have to think. My me-space is the bathroom. I can be alone, there—without interruption. I can settle myself, soak, or pray or just sink into the quiet side of my soul and refresh my thoughts and emotions. We need a place of utter peace. Call it a *woman-cave*—an in-house escape from the tedium that can infect our marriages. We need those moments when we can free ourselves from ourselves and experience a spiritual molting—a renewing of our minds to shed our agitated thoughts in exchange for loving ones. Remember when we were little girls pulling daisy petals from their stems: *He loves me, he loves me not?* We wanted the last petal to be *He loves me!* As women and wives, we still want that last confirming petal, but there are times when we feel like we are left holding *He loves me not*.

Like anything else, marriage can become routine. Too often, our days evolve into a series of scheduled events with every hour crammed with to-dos, our priorities self-directed. Insensitivities sour our conversations. Life issues sap our energy. Our clocks wind down too quickly leaving little pep for our marriages. If we do not take corrective action, distance (rather than oneness) settles in. We find ourselves wondering why our marriages are mundane, even lifeless; why our husbands are apathetic and unresponsive to our needs; why they show us little or no affection and cannot or will not break away from working, or the TV, or emailing, texting, tweeting, or endlessly Facebooking when we are trying to spend time with them. Worse than those frustrated wonderings is the anxiety that rises in us when we sense that our marriages are in real danger and our thoughts turn to fear. We are afraid of what might be and are deeply offended because we perceive that our husbands are indifferent toward us. We resent them for shirking their responsibilities, and feel insulted at the unloving way they speak and act toward us. We grieve their loss of interest in us, both physically and emotionally; and are suspicious of them, of their evasiveness. We wonder—painfully—are our husbands cheating on us? If not, why are they so cranky, selfish, unavailable, unreliable and—shall I say it?—boring? In fact, who are these people masquerading as the wonderful men we married?

It is not good enough to survive marriage, we should thrive in marriage. But that will not happen in an atmosphere of disharmony. Marriage is a duet. It requires two hearts performing as one, bringing a pleasing and consistent quality to the marriage relationship. But to be in tune with one another, to effect harmony, there must be a clear understanding of the parts each must play. The Bible defines our role as wives in Ephesians 5:22–23.

> *Wives, submit to your own husbands, as to the Lord. For the husband is head of the wife, as also Christ is head of the church; and He is the Savior of the body. Therefore, just as the church is subject to Christ, so let the wives be to their own husbands in everything.*

I can feel those red flags going up. *Submit!?* Submit to husbands who are not demonstrating headship? Yes. Remember, marriage is a duet. We should be on the same sheet with our husbands. If they stop playing, the music loses its quality. If we stop playing, too, there is no music. Since every marriage is unique, each of us has to determine where we are unsubmitted and work on those areas. For some of us, it means not nagging; for others, it means not being demanding; for all of us, it means getting out of the way and allowing our husbands to lead. It's not so prickly when we realize that the Bible calls our husbands to submission as well. They are commanded to love us solely and completely, as their duty to us.

> *Even so husbands should and are morally obligated to love their own wives as [being in a sense] their own bodies. He who loves his own wife loves himself. For no one ever hated his own body, but [instead] he nourishes and protects and cherishes it, just as Christ does the church, because we are members (parts) of His body.* (Ephesians 5:28–30 AMP)

When husbands cease to love us as they ought to and slip into behaviors that are manifestly uncaring, or mutate leadership into dictatorships, they belittle love. Love is freely given from a surrendered heart. It is not an assumption. It is not just a matter of saying, "I love you." Nor is it something to save for Valentine's Day, poetically scrolled across a Hallmark card. Those types of professions are nice, albeit passive. They are like sentimental lyrics: lovely to compose, but they must be sung to be a song. Love must be active—self-giving. Maybe our husbands should start remembering when they were grooms, when they were full of excitement for the life we would share. We could wait for that epiphanic moment to come; however, someone has to get the music started again while there is music to be had. We cannot sit idly by expecting our marriages to be vibrant with no effort from either side. Since our discussion is about growing as wives, that someone is us. We start by tamping down our feelings of offence (justified or not) and resurrecting the bride in us so that we can see the essential men we love through the junk of our marriage relationships. When we do this—when we look at our husbands through the eyes of a bride, we make it easier to engage that word we don't like and *submit* to them as leaders in our marriages. As we do that, we make it easier to strike a conciliatory note in our hearts which can change our attitudes, heal hurts, and inspire our husbands to do better—to be better. This is not a cop-out, and it is not placating bad behavior. It is reestablishing the duet. It is taking heroic measures through the storms of marriage to love as we ought to love. "To have a heroic marriage, you must become a heroic spouse, whether or not your mate does likewise," writes Al Jassen in *The Marriage Masterpiece*. "There are no shortcuts, simple steps, or easy gimmicks. It requires the courage to overcome pride and selfishness in order to lay down your life for another. Not because your spouse deserves it; he or she may not. Not because it will improve your relationship; it might not. You do it because you are part of something much bigger than yourself, and because you are called to reflect the Masterpiece of God."

That masterpiece is alive in us through the person of Jesus Christ, Who by His Spirit, is able to cleanse our hearts of negative emotions and resurrect our bride-memories. Those memories do not die because of marital discord; they dissipate—becoming as dull and dark as unpolished silver due to neglect, hostilities, disappointments, and plain old marriage fatigue. But we can make them sparkle again by remembering who we are in Christ and reacting to the challenges we face in our marriages through the witness of Galatians 2:20:

> *"I have been crucified with Christ; and it is no lon-*
> *ger I who live, but Christ lives in me; and the life*
> *which I now live in the flesh I live by faith in the Son*
> *of God, who loved me and gave Himself up for me."*
> *(NASB)*

Without Jesus Christ living in the center of our marriages and our hearts, our human love will not endure over the long haul through difficulties and disillusionments. We need a reason to rise above the mire of marriage, and it is our trust in the healing power of Jesus. Willing ourselves is futile because our will is tied to our emotions. We may not like the idea of setting aside our feelings and focusing on the promises we made when we were brides, but we need to do it. Sometimes that means pushing ourselves or getting an accountability partner or counselor to encourage us to press forward. We have to force those memories and commitments to the surface by arduously conditioning ourselves to live marriage by *The Book*, seeking the Lord and praying for our marriages, making sure we are well fed with the fruit of the Spirit by keeping a close connection with Jesus. Ladies, we cannot control our husbands nor are we supposed to; only God can do that. We are supposed to control ourselves. That we can do, and we have the assurance of Philippians 4:13, confirming in us that we can do *all* things through Christ Who strengthens us. We have to ignore our pride and call on Him when our feelings are inflamed, approaching God's throne of grace confidently, "so that we may receive mercy and find grace to help us in our time of need." (Hebrews 4:16 NIV) He knows what it will take to get our emotions back in shape so that we can love with the instincts of a bride and be one with our husbands when the challenges of married life occur. The best part is that Jesus is always available: our Teacher and Comforter. He does not charge a fee, and He guarantees results. His only requirement is that we seek Him.

> *Come to Me, all you who labor and are heavy laden, and I will give you rest. Take My yoke upon you and learn from Me, for I am gentle and lowly in heart, and you will find rest for your souls. For My yoke is easy and My burden is light.* (Matthew 11:38–30)

Working Out Oneness

What was your dream about the kind of wedding you wanted?

_____

How much of your "dream wedding" was a dream come true?

_____

Did you have wedding day jitters? Did they rise to a level of fear regarding what you were about to do? If yes, what did you do about them?

_____

What was your concept then about married life with your husband?

_____

Was your concept realistic or unrealistic?

_____

Would you say you were like King Solomon, in love with love, or did you come to the altar with a clearheaded love?

_____

When you repeated your wedding vows, how much understanding did you have that you were entering into a covenant with God as well as with your husband?

_____

Looking back, do you wish you had planned your wedding differently? If so, what changes would you make? Would you scrap the wedding and have a family-only ceremony, keep the wedding but spend less money on it, spend more money on it, use the money for a downpayment on a house, or something else?

_____

Where was Christ on the day of your wedding? Was He in the service, your thoughts, your words, or your heart?

_____

What is the most memorable part of your wedding experience?

_____

How much of your bride-perspective is still alive in you?

_____

An Excellent Wife Is the Crown of Her Husband

(Proverbs 12:4)

To Love and to Cherish

Never is true love blind, but rather brings an added
light; an inner vision quick to find; the beauties
hid from common sight.
Phoebe Cary

Being in love is the closest we come to weightlessness with-out floating in a spacecraft headed for the stars. It's as if we are being swept away on an inner wind, softly, powerfully. We feel lighter, freer, and happier. Every aspect of our being is different than before—better than before. Fueled by our sys-tem's very own propellant—an intoxicating blend of dopamine, adrenaline, and norepinephrine—we soar with thoughts of love. So much has been written, said, and sung about love from time immemorial. And yet, all of us come to love in our own unique way. One of the most vibrant depictions of romantic love is found in Song of Solomon 8:6–7:

> *Place me like a seal over your heart,*
> *like a seal on your arm;*
> *for love is as strong as death,*
> *its jealousy unyielding as the grave.*
> *It burns like blazing fire,*
> *like a mighty flame.*
> *Many waters cannot quench love;*
> *rivers cannot sweep it away.*

If one were to give
all the wealth of one's house for love,
it would be utterly scorned. (NIV)

It would be hard to find a more passionate outpouring of love than these words spoken by the Shulammite to her beloved. She is unabashedly passionate about her love for him, yet her speech, though remarkably unrestrained, is not sordid. It is pure. There is nothing that she would exchange for her love for him: not wealth or any earthly treasure, because as much as she loves him, she cherishes him as well.

What is interesting here is that in Ecclesiastes 5:28–29, the apostle Paul admonishes *husbands* to cherish their wives, "So husbands ought to love their own wives as their own bodies; he who loves his wife loves himself. For no one ever hated his own flesh, but nourishes it and cherishes it, just as the Lord does the church." This is not a message for wives. Yet, when we repeated our wedding vows, not only did we pledge to love our husbands, we pledged to cherish them also. The fact that Paul is not speaking to us does not mean that our vows to our husbands are in conflict with Scripture or that they are less significant. The Greek word for cherish is *thalpei*. It means "to warm." The moment we vowed to cherish our husbands, we made a promise to show them warmth through love. The Shulammite says that her love "burns like a blazing fire, like a mighty flame." When we think back to the time when we were brides, we find that we were like a mighty flame, too, burning for our husbands-to-be. All our thoughts toward them were warm, because we cherished them.

There is a reason that love and cherish are important aspects of the ceremonial question: "Do you promise to love and to cherish?" Both words are essential and of separate but equal value; they are interdependent. Think of it this way: If love is a mighty fire, then cherish is the energy that keeps it burning. If we reduce the amount of energy, we reduce the intensity of the fire. In other words, we lose our heat, our love cools, and if we are not careful, our fire goes out and love dies.

Heat matters in a marriage. So why do we stop cherishing our husbands as we did when we answered, "I do?" I suppose it happens gradually, when we are no longer brides but wives. We get caught up with the demands of expected and unexpected frustrations, discontent and worries, sometimes for years. We can forget that there was a time when we were like the Shulammite woman—that our love was a burning flame. The thing about a flame though is that it doesn't take much to extinguish it—even a mighty flame. A shift in the air, smothering words, a dousing of distrust; each can quench a flame. It is not enough to be in love. Lasting love, like fire, needs to be energized if it is to give lifelong warmth. That's why love and cherish are separate but equal and interdependent. We have to stoke our love with our thoughts, the kind we had toward our husbands when we married them and cherished them. Our love will not burn on its own any more than a damp log will catch fire. We have to coax it whether we want to or not, whether we have warm feelings for our husbands or not. Otherwise, we will never move forward in our relationships with them. We might as well turn a fire hose on our love. I do not pretend that it is easy. It is not. It is hard work. It is humbling. But it is necessary, because what I know for certain is that it is impossible to cherish our husbands when we harbor anger and unforgiveness toward them. So how do we do it? We ignite our bride-memories. If this is the point where you say to yourselves, "Seriously? No way." I get it. Sometimes, trying to live with our husbands is all we can manage. Digging through old memories is as exciting as cleaning cobwebs from the attic, especially when our marriages are covered in the dust of unresolved issues. It can seem like too much effort much too late. But the Bible says, "If God is for us, who can be against us?" (Romans 8:31) We need to go to Him Who is "our refuge and strength, a very present help in trouble." (Psalm 46:1) He is able to free us from the things that prey on our minds and hold us back. He is able to save us from the snare of emotional bondage, which inevitably leads to bitterness, pridefulness—or, just as erosive: indifference. A favorite Bible verse of mine is Isaiah 43:18–19, "Forget the former things; do not dwell on the past. See, I am doing a new thing! Now it springs up; do you not perceive it? I am making a way in the wilderness and streams in the wasteland." I hung on these words many times when marital bliss felt more like a painful blister.

There is another reason that *love* and *cherish* have equal importance in a healthy marriage. Though they are separate aspects of the marriage relationship, they must function as one heart, just as husbands and wives live as one flesh. Maintaining that oneness of heart is part of the work of marriage. We can love our husbands and not cherish them. We do this when we take them for granted or focus too much of our attention on other things or other people, or on the things we consider to be their faults. We cherish what we regard as special or meaningful, that which touches us in a particular, often tender or sentimental way. We cherish the people or things we hold dear. For example, we might love our mother's apple pie, but we do not cherish it. What we cherish is the recipe for the pie, which has been a family treasure for generations. The principle is the same when it comes to our husbands. We love them. But we cherish the unique qualities that reflect their natures or personalities—treasures that are found only in them. When love and cherish are working in unison, our love is made whole, and we are in alignment with God's will for our marriages. Cherish is love actualized, and love actualized is God's heart. In 1 John 4:7, it says, "Beloved, let us love one another, for love is of God: and everyone who loves is born of God and knows God."

When we are brides, we are deeply in love with our husbands-to-be and want nothing more than to close the door on the world and surround ourselves with them. In the ancient Greek language, our feelings are best described as *eros*. It is the kind of love that is passionate, intimate, and adoring. We are hardwired to experience passion and to desire intimacy, both sexual and emotional. However, God's highest standard for expressing love in a marriage is *agape* because it is unconditional love; it is not dependent on our feelings. Agape is intentional love, the type found in 1 Corinthians 13:4–7. This love is long suffering and kind; it is patient, not envious, boastful, or proud; it is not rude or easily angered; it is not self-seeking nor does it keep a record of wrongs or delight in evil but rejoices with truth. It bears all things, believes all things, hopes all things, and endures all things. This message is counterintuitive to our reflexive natures when we feel slighted, ignored, or unappreciated by our husbands. But it is how Jesus loves us when we exhibit the same behaviors and attitudes toward Him. We cannot accomplish this depth of love over the course of married life if we do not cherish our husbands. But when we do, we keep our warmth, and where there is warmth there is fire—maybe not a blaze; a flame, perhaps, or even a flicker will do because it burns with hope

We've talked a lot about warmth as the defining element for giving meaning to the word *cherish*. But what we have not discussed is the role gratitude plays in creating these warm, cherishing feelings that bind our hearts to the men we love. The story of Mary, the mother of Jesus, has much to tell us about this facet of love. Before her immaculate conception, Mary was a typical young woman of her era, eagerly waiting for the day when her betrothal would become a completed union with her beloved, Joseph. By Jewish custom, Mary's betrothal took place several months prior to her wedding day, and only after Joseph had presented her parents (in particular, her father) with an acceptable ketubah . The *ketubah* is a legal and binding marriage contract, which details the obligations of the husband to his wife. It is a requisite document ensuring that a wife (in this case, Mary) is protected and supported, and that her emotional and physical needs are met. Unlike a promise of marriage or an official engagement typical of a modern-day proposal, a *betrothal* is a covenant equivalent to our marriage vows. In effect, a betrothal *is* a marriage. So once Joseph presented an acceptable ketubah, he would have said to Mary, "By this, thou art set apart for me according to the laws of Moses and of Israel." With those few words, Mary became a married woman bonded to Joseph in every way, except sexually. Consummation would take place later, on the wedding day, followed by a celebration or feast. Although the allotted time for planning the wedding celebration was different in custom and meaning from our engagement period, the months of preparation leading up to the big day abounded with the same excitement, expectancy, and happiness that couples enjoy today! This was a joyful time for putting things in order: for Joseph to secure the finances needed to support the marriage, for Mary's parents to organize the wedding festivities, and for Mary to select her bridal attire.

It was during this time that the angel Gabriel visited Mary and said, "Rejoice, highly favored one, the Lord is with you, blessed are you among women!" What an incredible moment for Mary! We don't know what Gabriel looked like, but we know that he was not an apparition; he appeared as a man. (Daniel 8:15, 9:21)

But what kind of a man? Was he tall, handsome, muscular? Was he incandescent? For certain, his was not a familiar face. Mary was taken aback. That much is clearly spelled out in Luke 1:29. Gabriel calmed her by saying, "Do not be afraid, Mary, for you have found favor with God."

It is not difficult to imagine the thoughts that were swirling in Mary's head. She was very young. In biblical times, it was customary for a girl to be eligible for marriage when she reached twelve years of age or had experienced her first menstrual cycle. So Mary was not a sophisticated adult woman at the time of Gabriel's visit. By our standards, she was a child. Maybe she was alone in her room or outside in the garden when, out of nowhere, Gabriel appeared before her. Is it any wonder she was taken aback? Yet, amazingly, she handled herself with poise—no yelling, crying, or running to her parents.

Let me digress for just a moment to say that timing and grace are crucial to a good response. There was violence against women in Mary's day just as there is today. How many of us would be as composed as she when confronted by a strange man who popped up out of nowhere? I would not, and I have an embarrassing record of proof. Ephesians 4:7 says that "to each one of us grace was given according to the measure of Christ's gift." I don't know the number of my measure, but I have had times of needing more. I will never forget the moment when I was so stunned by the sudden appearance of an unexpected man that I instantly and completely lost whatever measure of grace I was given. It just shot right out of me the way breath leaves our bodies when struck with great force. Morris and I were having some roofing work done on our house. Every morning for about a week a crew of roofers came to do the repairs. One morning, I was upstairs dressing, preparing to leave the house for an appointment. Stevie (that's what we called our son when he was young), was about five years old then. Unbeknownst to me, he had let one of the roofers into the house, ostensibly to use our first floor bathroom. When I came downstairs, I decided (as we women often do) to give myself one last hair and makeup check. I went to the bathroom, pulled open the door, comb in hand, and stood face-to-face with the roofer—a six-foot plus guy who was not in a position to receive an audience. I froze in place with a raised comb and began screaming. He shot up from the toilet seat to a half-stance and froze too, obviously shocked, his pants gathered around his knees. I slammed the door shut and ran upstairs, hoping to avoid him. When I thought enough time had passed for him to have left the house, I went downstairs. He must have been waiting for me to leave the house as well, because just as I was entering the hallway, he was coming out of the bathroom. We ran right into each other. I apologized to him profusely. He never came into the house again. I could not believe I reacted to his surprising presence by screaming.

God knew Mary would not become hysterical at the unexpected sight of Gabriel, however terrifying his appearance. He had already given her enough grace to receive him and his message. So she listened as he continued speaking to her, saying, "And behold, you will conceive in your womb and bring forth a Son, and shall call His name Jesus. He will be great, and will be called the Son of the Highest, and the Lord God will give Him the throne of His father David. And He will reign over the house of Jacob forever, and of His kingdom there will be no end." Mary asked Gabriel, "How can this be, since I do not know a man?" Gabriel replied, "The Holy Spirit will come upon you, and the power of the Highest will overshadow you; therefore, also, that Holy One Who is to be born will be called the Son of God." When he finished delivering the message that God had entrusted to him, Mary said, "Behold the maidservant of the Lord! Let it be to me according to your word." (Luke 1:31–38)

In today's world, it is not unheard of for a man to marry a woman who is pregnant with another man's child and, because he loves her, choose to raise the child as his own. But in Nazareth, more than 2,000 years ago, a married woman (which is what Mary was technically) in such a condition was considered an adulteress and likely to be stoned.

For reasons that are not clear, Mary decided to travel to the hill country to visit her cousin Elizabeth in Judah. Perhaps it was because she was eager to see the miracle that God was performing within Elizabeth and be assured that, with God, nothing is impossible. Gabriel had already explained to her that Elizabeth, an old woman past the age of childbearing, was going to have a child and was six-months pregnant with baby John, later to be known as John the Baptist. (Luke 1:36–37) This had to be thrilling news to Mary and a compelling reason for her to visit Elizabeth. Yes, they were relatives, and it appears that they were fond of one another; but they were very different women, more like aunt and niece, considering the disparity of years between them. Yet, because of the unparalleled life growing in their wombs, they were venerable peers, divinely connected by God.

Mary remained with Elizabeth for three months before returning home. Joseph must have been ecstatic to see her, but his joy was to come to an abrupt halt as he learned that his betrothed was carrying someone else's child. (Matthew 1:19) This was the kind of report that caused men of his day to tear their clothes and heap ashes on their heads in a public display of grief and humiliation. But Joseph was a "just man." (Matthew 1:19) He decided to protect Mary's name by securing a discrete divorce. This had to have been an emotional struggle for him.

Even though he was a just man, he was still a man and husband to Mary; and any husband, in any culture or point in time, would find a story like Mary's—of an immaculate conception—hard to swallow. "But while he thought about these things, behold, an angel of the Lord appeared to him in a dream saying, "Joseph, son of David, do not be afraid to take to you Mary your wife, for that which is conceived in her is of the Holy Spirit. And she will bring forth a Son, and you shall call His name Jesus, For He will save His people from their sins." (Matthew 1:20–21)

There is a difference between Mary's experience with Gabriel and Joseph's experience with an angel of the Lord. Gabriel came to Mary in person. The angel of the Lord came to Joseph in a dream. It seems to me that it was because Joseph had a strong faith in God that he didn't discount the dream as a figment of his bewildered mind. Instead, he "did as the angel of the Lord commanded him and took to him his wife." (Matthew 1:20–21, 24) This leads me to believe that Mary and Joseph loved and cherished each other. Even before the angel of the Lord appeared to Joseph, he demonstrated how much he loved and cherished Mary by seeking to protect her reputation, though her circumstance, as he perceived it, was greatly dishonoring to him. By taking Mary as his wife, he endured ridicule from the townspeople, protected Mary from their scorn, and saved her Son from the hatred of King Herod who sought to kill Jesus. Is there any doubt that Mary, in return, loved her protector and cherished his strength of character and his faithfulness in obeying the promptings of God? Mary's bride-memories must have glowed with warmth and gratefulness every time she reflected on her hero husband. Could it be that a lesson we should take from Mary's story is that the way we cherish our husbands is an outward expression of gratefulness and a confirmation of how much we value them? This could be a challenging concept in the face of our fast-paced, me-oriented world where so much is assumed.

But not everyone is motivated by worldly assumptions. This was made crystal clear by the sober perspective of Adrienne. To meet her is to feel immediately at ease. She has the kind of face that lights up when she smiles, and when she speaks about how she cherishes her husband, Jeffrey, her softly-spoken words flow out of her like a low tide—a gentle stream of tender thoughts that convey experience, love, and maturity.

> *It's critical for us to cherish our husbands. It's important for them to feel good about who they are and what they bring to the marriage. I cherish the fact that Jeffrey adds things to my life that I wouldn't have but for him, and that brings value to our life, marriage, and home.*
>
> *I cherish his passion and independence as well as the things we do together. I love how excited he gets about things that make him feel like a better person. It can be running or cycling or a new chapter in the Bible. It's that passion that he has about life that helps us experience things in a fresh way and keeps us from getting into a rut. We get to appreciate things together, with new eyes. If you don't keep blowing on the spark, it goes out.*

In other words: oneness. Adrienne experiences oneness every time she actualizes her love for Jeffrey by the ways she cherishes him. She is wedded to the dual effect that is symbiotic to love and cherish, which, like identical twins, is birthed from the same parent emotion and particularized by their different names. But she says that it is more than that.

> It's also what you show the world about your feelings toward a person. Men look for outside value, for how others view them. Jeffery needs that kind of affirmation. I hear it when he talks. He always wants to say, "Look, come see what I'm doing!"

Adrienne giggles, and for an instant, a glimpse of a blushing young girl from years past invades her otherwise poised demeanor.

> This sounds silly, I know (her giggle entangles her words). Jeffrey likes it when I post messages about him on social media. He likes the little personal notes that I send through Facebook and other social media. He'll come back and say, "Thank you for saying that." He wants other people to know I appreciate him. And when we are around other people, and I comment about him by saying things like, "Jeffrey did this or Jeffrey did that," I can see him stand taller. He looks to see how I respond to him. The more he sees that I appreciate the things that matter to him, the more effort he puts into it, whether it's something around the house or outside the house, I see him exploring how he can make whatever it is better. And that's not just for me; he's growing from it.

She admits that there are times when the weight of oneness is heavy and the work hard. All the more reason for us to remember when we were brides, vowing to love and cherish the precious men we were so excited to marry.

> *It's not that disappointments never come, but when they come, we have to step back and look at the situation from the view of a third party. Separating ourselves from that moment is helpful in keeping perspective. We have to ask ourselves the question: "Does this moment overshadow how I cherish this person?" Love is an ember. Cherishing keeps the ember alive.*

There is a verse in 1 Peter that provides us with God's point of view on what it means *to love and to cherish till death do us part*: "And above all things have fervent love for one another, for love will cover a multitude of sins." (4:8) The question is, Are we willing to love that fervently to the end? With God's help, we can do it. We can dust off our bride-memories and revive those warm, cherishing feelings that have dimmed to a flicker, and turn them into a flame. I repeat: It is work—work that must be continued. Having done it (in fact, I am still doing it), I can say with all sincerity and faith in the Lord Jesus—without Whom I could not do it—that it is work that works.

Working Out Oneness

In what ways do you actively work at expressing love for your husband?

_____

Can you list five characteristics about his nature which you cherish? Are they the same ones you cherished when you married him?

_____

How important is it to cherish your husband? In your experience, how do you distinguish it from loving him?

_____

In what way do you express gratefulness to God for the gift of your husband?

_____

To what extent do love and cherish express oneness in your marriage?

Considering that to cherish someone represents warmth in the relationship, how warm is your marriage? What is the intensity of your love for your husband?

Mary had many reasons to love Joseph, but if there was one attribute she cherished more than anything else, it would be his strength of character. What one trait do you cherish above all others in your husband?

Do you ever feel that your love is cooling? What precipitated the change and what are you doing about it?

What are the problem areas in your marriage that throw cold water on your warm feeling toward your husband?

———————————————————————————————

Do you ever revisit the feelings you had toward your husband, when you were a bride?

———————————————————————————————

Which type of love is stronger in you when it comes to loving and cherishing your husband: agape or Eros?

———————————————————————————————

To what extent do you think your husband feels valued by you, because of the way you love and cherish him?

———————————————————————————————

For Better or for Worse

And be kind to one another, tenderhearted, forgiving one another, even as God in Christ forgave you.
(Ephesians 4:32)

Some things cannot be fully understood except by blunt experience. It is easy to embrace *better*—but *worse*? I cannot imagine any bride repeating her wedding vows, contemplating the bad things that sometimes happen to marriages, especially things that traumatize—things like unfaithfulness, financial ruin, profound illness, indifference, lack of intimacy, or, most egregious: abuse, either physical or emotional. With thoughts like these, who would ever risk marriage? Weddings are our greatest public expression of love, trust, and oneness. They represent a time of joy and optimism, not just for the wedding day, but for the rest of our lives as women, as wives, as members of society. When we pledge that we will be with our husbands for better or for worse, we are making a profession of faith.

Now faith is the substance of things hoped for, the evidence of things not seen. (Hebrews 11:2)

If we believe the Word of God, then we must also believe that God desires that we have great marriages as much—if not more—than we do. Where we get into trouble is in prioritizing our ways over His ways. God is the Master designer of marriage.

His priority for marriage is always the same: oneness. He said as much in Genesis 2:24, "Therefore a man shall leave his father and mother and be joined to his wife, and they shall become one flesh." He wants us to uphold our wedding vows and prosper in our marriages through mutual love and faith in each other, in Him, and in the sanctity of marriage.

Faith and love go hand-in-hand. Both emanate from God the Father through Jesus Christ. Both are essential if we are to experience marriage as God proposed. This mingling of faith and love is the essence of real love. It is divine, spiritual, and reasoned. It is the same love that God has for us. When we love His way, we choose to love our husbands freely and sacrificially, just as God chose to love us freely and sacrificially by sending Jesus to die for us so that we could be saved from eternal death. Without His kind of love, which imparts faith to love, we lose God's purpose for marriage. We forget how enamored we were as brides and unwittingly give space for Satan to slip into our midst and compromise our marriage relationships with selfish thoughts, selfish acts, and hostile words. These compromises, by their very nature and source, are designed to destroy what God has put together. They are the little foxes spoken of in the Bible that have grown big and strong.

> Catch us the foxes, the little foxes that spoil the vines, for our vines have tender grapes. (Song of Solomon 2:15)

We need faith to love our husbands for better or for worse. But here is the crux of the matter: Married love is a covenant we make with our husbands and with God. Therefore, we have an obligation to uphold it. So what does covenantal love look like? In 1 Corinthians 13:4–7, it was laid out plainly: "Love suffers long and is kind; love does not envy; love does not parade itself, is not puffed up; does not behave rudely, does not seek its own, is not provoked, thinks no evil; does not rejoice in iniquity, but rejoices in the truth; bears all things, believes all things, hopes all things, endures all things." Would it sound too pessimistic if I modified the advice I gave to my daughters when they were getting married to say, "This kind of love is the hardest work we ever do, if we are to keep our promises"? I don't mean to be discouraging—just honest. Life contends with sacrificial love and what we know to be true in God. This kind of love cost Jesus His life. It costs us as well. But we don't marry with the cost of love on our minds. We love because it is who we are. We were created in the likeness of God, and God is love. It is our sin nature that rails against that fact; and it is our sin nature that goes with us into our marriages and makes us vulnerable to destructive attitudes and behaviors that reflect our enemy more than our Friend, stirring passions that are anything but romantic or loving. This is true for both husbands and wives.

Case in point: I was driving home one day, listening to a Christian radio station. Chuck Swindoll was speaking. His message was taken from the series *Looking Ahead to Things That Last*. I have always enjoyed his broadcasts, but this time, he really got my attention with a funny, sardonic tale about a confrontation with Satan.

> *One bright beautiful Sunday morning the townspeople were in church listening to the organ playing when suddenly, Satan appeared at the front of the church and everyone started screaming and running for the front entrance or the back entrance, every exit they could get out. They were trampling each other in a frantic effort to get away from evil*

incarnate. Soon everyone was evacuated from the church except for one old gentleman who sat calmly in his pew, not moving, seemingly oblivious to the fact that God's ultimate enemy was in his presence. This sort of confused Satan. So he walked over to the old man and said, "Don't you know who I am?"

The old man replied, "Yep. Sure do."
Satan asked, "Aren't you afraid of me?"
"Nope. Sure ain't," said the old man.
Satan was a little perturbed at this and asked, "Why aren't you afraid of me?"
The old man replied, "I've been married to your sister for 48 years."

So much of what we experience as stress in our marriages could be ameliorated, if not eliminated, by effective premarital counseling by a trained Christian counselor who can articulate the principles of building a successful marriage. My mother used to say, "The way you begin is the way you end up." It was an admonition in the form of an adage to illustrate the choices we have in building a marriage. We can build one that is happy and stable—one that endures and is mutually gratifying; or, we can build one that is miserable and unstable—one that brings heart- ache and ruin. The choice is ours, but our marriages will stand or collapse on the strength of their foundations. In Matthew 7:24–27, Jesus used a parable to explain what happens when we build on a strong foundation, or on a weak one. "Therefore everyone who hears these words of mine and puts them into practice is like a wise man who built his house on the rock. The rain came down, the streams rose, and the winds blew and beat against that house; yet it did not fall, because it had its foundation on the rock. But everyone who hears these words of mine and does not put them into practice is like a foolish man who built his house on sand. The rain came down, the streams rose, and the winds blew and beat against that house, and it fell with a great crash."

Many of us marry in churches for the reverential atmosphere but do not have the benefit of good, Christian counseling to take with us when the service is over and our "I dos" are behind us. And even when counseling is available and welcomed, it can be devoid of meaningful instruction for understanding how to work through the hard stuff that comes to all married couples. I will never forget the superficial advice I was given when Morris and I went for premarriage counseling with Father Parker, the priest presiding over our church. Referring to my role in keeping my husband happy and my marriage secure, he said I should be a lady in the living room, a chef in the kitchen, and a hussy in the bedroom. That was the sum and sad truth of his counsel to me. I was dumbstruck and embarrassed. I felt like I was being interviewed for a job as a waitress in a strip joint. I don't think he meant to be offensive. I am sure he said what he was accustomed to saying. Who knows how many times he shared his three-point plan for marital bliss with other young women, thinking he was offering sage advice? Perhaps his chauvinistic perspective was a peek into how he defined his wife, if not an unintended leak from his own unfulfilled needs. Suffice to say, his counsel was not helpful.

When I think about the first years of my marriage (even some subsequent years), and the difficulties of being one with my husband, I have to admit that there were many times when I could have written lyrics to the Tina Turner song: "What's Love Got to Do with It"! Today, couples have a different refrain for their marital frustrations: *"I didn't sign up for this!"* Every generation has quips for coping when life becomes stressful. I still remember many that were favorites of my parents when I was growing up. They were a kind of medicine, like stinging iodine, for just about any situation that needed a verbal cure. "Keep the pot boiling" was one of those old expressions that combined warning and wisdom in a few words. It is a home-spun allusion to a wife's responsibility when it comes to car-ing for her husband and family, and dates back to the sixteenth century. It implies that when the pot is boiling, something must be in it that can be eaten. Figuratively, it's an abbreviated les-son in conflict avoidance, or more literally: how to be prepared for whatever comes. My conclusion? If one pot is sufficient for either interpretation, imagine what two or three boiling pots could accomplish! But I am ahead of myself.

Morris and I grew up in the same city, about a mile from one another. We went to some of the same schools, the same church, and our parents were close friends. But our households were very different. His parents seemed to stick closely to their respective roles. My parents crossed the divide in certain ways. For example, though my mother was an excellent cook and prepared the primary family meals, my father also enjoyed cooking, particularly ethnic foods. It was not unusual for him to decide on a whim to make a big pot of pasta fazool or yaka-mein, and on an occasional Sunday, salt mackerel served with pan-roasted potatoes and onions. His cooking was sporadic: If he could throw his craving into a pot, he would coddle it until it succumbed to a tasty dish. And he made a mean sandwich with a fat slice of kosher dill pickle on the side. My husband's father was the complete opposite. His relationship with food was in eating it—a legacy preserved in my husband as if it had been encoded through some fantastic feat of gene-splicing. We had barely settled into our life together when food became an issue in our marriage. Our first apartment was in a house in the neighborhood where I grew up, about two blocks from my parents' home. To say that it was an apartment is a stretch—it consisted of three furnished rooms on the second floor of the house. We did not have an eat-in kitchen or dining room. Instead, there was a cutout in the wall between the kitchen and our bedroom—a square opening, like a window, just big enough to be functional for food service. The kitchen was so small that the two of us could not be in it at the same time nor could I open the oven door without stepping to the side of it first. In the bedroom, there was a small walnut-stained table with two chairs nestled against either end of it; the stove was directly opposite the table on the kitchen side of the wall. I would cook the food, plate it, and pass it through the opening to my husband seated at the table. Being the new bride that I was, it seemed perfect for us—a tiny, cozy love nest reminiscent of a Manhattan efficiency apartment.

Not so perfect were some of Morris's mealtime habits. I admit up front that the fruit of my spirit was lacking in patience. However, it was astonishing to me that a grown man would come to the table, daily, and ask, "Is my food the right temperature?" I am certain my daily response was just as astonishing to him. I would reply, "How would I know if your food is the right temperature for you? You will have to taste it." His other favorite question was, "Does this need salt?" Though not exactly a category eater, he preferred all elements of his meal to be categorically separated. I was to be careful when serving a second helping of one food that it did not encroach on the forbidden territory of another food. It could be a crisis if the peas were found in the potato section or vice versa. Keep in mind that I was twenty-one years old, ignorant of food idiosyncrasies, and sorely devoid of tact. But I tried to be a sensitive wife, sometimes to my chagrin. I can recall with humor now the time I nearly ruined his breakfast. Being a creature of habit, he wanted scrambled eggs (hard) with bacon and toast every morning. I noticed that as soon as I passed his plate to him, he would pick up his fork and begin mashing the scrambled eggs. One morning I decided that I would do that for him and serve his breakfast the way he liked it. I mashed the scrambled eggs with a fork and gave him his plate. He looked at it and said, "What did you do to my eggs?" I said, "I mashed them for you." Exasperated, he said, "Why did you do that? Now I have to mash them all over again!" With his fork in hand as if a pronged spear, he proceeded to mash the eggs a second time. When he finished, his twice-mashed eggs looked like a thick covering of pollen spread about his plate. Clearly, we were not off to a great start.

During the first year, we moved to a real apartment. The kitchen was almost as small as the previous one but much more open. There was a dining room adjacent to it which made the overall space more accessible. This time we had our own dining table with seating for four. It was a garden-style table made of moss green wrought iron on which a lightly tinted glass top rested. I thought it gave a lovely, airy feeling to the room—a decided change from what we had in our first living arrangement for our dining pleasure. But the new environment did not alter the mealtime routine, and my attitude was not improving either. I got sick of trying to anticipate Morris's meal preferences, getting his dinner on his plate, on the table, exactly when he specified: at 5:30 p.m. Sometimes he didn't get home from work early enough to eat at the prescribed hour because he was detained or he missed the bus. Cell phones didn't exist, then. I would run back and forth from the kitchen to the living room widow watching for him, watching the food, moving it in and out of the oven, trying to keep it from overcooking and drying out. When he was at home on time, he would putter around the apartment, going through his end-of-workday rituals before coming to the table. The irony was that I liked to cook and I wanted to cook for him, but I started to hate the whole process of planning and preparing for mealtime. The daily ordeal of putting something in front of him at the right time, at the right temperature, with the right seasoning, and in the right food order burned away every bit of enthusiasm I had for cooking and serving a meal. After a while, I moved on to plan B—*Keep the pots boiling.* Though he was adamant that 5:30 p.m. was to be his dinner time, I figured he would be content if he saw that the meal was in preparation and almost on the table. So unbeknownst to him, at about the time he was due to return home, I would fill several pots with water and put them on the stove to boil. I kept lids on the pots, knowing he would never bother to lift them to see what was cooking. Remember, his connection to food was in consuming it; cooking it was my responsibility. When he entered the apartment, the steam from the bubbling pots gave the comforting message that dinner was imminent. It gave me relief from feeling like I was in a rerun episode of *I Love Lucy,* trying to keep my Ricky happy. Sounds crazy—right? But for me then it was emotional survival because I could count on the litany of complaints: It wasn't at the right time, it wasn't the right temperature, it didn't have the right amount of salt or pepper or whatever he wanted or didn't want. And I didn't have the right amount of Jesus working in me. It seemed to me that I could not do anything right when it came to serving a meal. The boiling pots gave me some peace of mind and a break from trying to gauge when he would finish his after-work routine and be ready to sit down at the table and eat.

It is true that, for me, the constant issues around food were maddening. In reality, they were about unexpected differences—part of the tapestry that was ours to work and weave, blending the diverse textures and tones of our individual personalities into one indestructible fabric. The problem that I had to face— despite what I disliked about the mealtime issues—was that I saw our differences as divisions—lines of contention that were intolerable and could not be crossed. Instead of working them out, or better yet, praying about them, I let them become my little foxes.

Sooner or later, every married couple comes face-to-face with little foxes. They prowl about in the shadows of our relationships; their presence is always destructive. Foxes are opportunists. They are nocturnal and territorial, carefully staking out their boundaries so that they can carry on undetected in the dark of night. This is how the little foxes of our marriages operate. They find a dark area in our thoughts and hang out there, gnawing on our frustrations, growing fat on our emotions. They never leave on their own. We must catch them and expel them or be consumed by them.

Michal could attest to that fact, if she were alive today to talk about it. She had firsthand experience with being outfoxed. (1 Samuel 18, 2 Samuel, and 1 Chronicles) Though her marriage to David happened more than 3,000 years ago, the passions that ruined her marriage are no different than the ones at work today. Ruin is what we risk when we fail to close the gate to our emotions: the little foxes run riot. Michal gave them freedom to scavenge in her mind. They found a place of darkness in her soul and began feeding on her bitterness toward David.

The destruction of her marriage happened gradually, as with most marriages. We know that she was deeply in love when she began her marriage to David and was fully committed to him. She literally saved his life by creating a plan of escape for him, away from the murderous schemes of her mentally unstable father, King Saul. She put her own position and well-being in jeopardy by hoodwinking her father's soldiers into believing that David was ill and, therefore, could not stand before the king as was being demanded of him. In truth, she had helped David escape from Saul through a window. But, by all appearances, he was lying in his sickbed, too weak to get up. Michal had placed a *teraph, a* large human-shaped figure representing a household idol, under the covers. To the unknowing soldiers, it looked like David's ailing body. When Saul realized that Michal had put one over on him and that David was gone, he challenged her, "Why have you deceived me like this, and sent my enemy away, so that he has escaped?" Still protecting the love of her life, she responded with a bold-faced lie, "He said to me, 'Let me get away. Why should I kill you?'" (1 Samuel 19)

Sometime later, Saul gave Michal to another man. His name was Paltiel. (1 Samuel 25:44) Years passed with no contact or communication between David to Michal. David was not searching for her or sending undercover agents to let her know that he loved her and would rescue her. He was on the run, staying out of Saul's reach and finding comfort in other women who would become his wives. After Saul died, David decided he wanted Michal returned to him. "So David sent messengers to Ishbosheth, Saul's son, saying, 'Give me my wife Michal, whom I betrothed to myself for a hundred foreskins of the Philistines.'" When the envoy showed up to take Michal, poor Paltiel was so distraught that he followed behind her weeping until he was sent away. (2 Samuel 3:14–15)

The Bible doesn't tell us what it was like for Michal living with Paltiel as his wife. But clearly, she had built a life with him, perhaps even learned to love him despite the manner in which she was given to him. What is ironic about her life is that it was love that first characterized her, and it was love that was twice snatched from her. She lost both the husband she loved and the husband who loved her. She must have felt completely powerless, angry, and victimized, initially by her father and then by David, making her ideal prey for a spirit of bitterness and a perfect habitat for little foxes. We can imagine her thought processes every time David did or said something that irritated her. After all, she was a wounded woman, and true to the age-old prerogative we women hold dear, she forgot nothing: neither the good nor the bad. Old anger would become like a field of weeds entangling her emotions. She would remember the fierce love she once felt for her handsome young warrior, the excitement that used to sweep over her every time he was near, the glorious day when she became his bride, and the warmth of his last embrace, as she helped him through a window so that he could escape her crazed father. She would remember her feelings of abandonment during the years she never heard from him, and the moment her father gave her to another man, even though she was still married to David, whom she loved. And, still fresh in her mind would be the outrage of her abduction from her home with Paltiel, which ripped her from his love (probably against her will, definitely against his), just because David wanted her back. Resentment and unforgiveness must have clawed at her mind as she regarded her new life, not as David's one and only wife, but one among his many wives and concubines. Ultimately, his insensitivity, his brashness, and the power he had over her collided with her rage, and on the day that David brought the ark back to Jerusalem and danced wildly before all the people, she seethed.

Watching from the window, she was disgusted by what she saw. The little foxes had grown big and strong. Anger had descended into bitterness toward David, exploding into disdainful words that destroyed what was left of her marriage. "How the king of Israel has distinguished himself today, going around half-naked in full view of the slave girls of his servants as any vulgar fellow would!" she said. David responded, "It was before the LORD, who chose me rather than your father or anyone from his house when he appointed me ruler over the LORD's people Israel—I will celebrate before the LORD. I will become even more undignified than this, and I will be humiliated in my own eyes. But by these slave girls you spoke of, I will be held in honor." (2 Samuel 6:20–22 NIV) From that point on, whatever bond existed between them was severed. There was no marriage relationship, no intimacy, and no love between them. "And Michal the daughter of Saul had no children to the day of her death." (2 Samuel 6:23 NIV)

Healthy marriages are work. They are molded by a mutual determination to uphold the marriage vows and love completely, forgivingly, and faithfully according to the tenets of 1 Corinthians 13:4–8, which bears repeating: "Love suffers long and is kind; love does not envy; love does not parade itself, is not puffed up; does not behave rudely, does not seek its own, is not provoked, thinks no evil; does not rejoice in iniquity, but rejoices in the truth; bears all things, believes all things, hopes all things, endures all things. Love never fails." Without question, this is the toughest kind of love to sustain between two completely different people over the span of a lifetime. Pragmatically speaking, it means that we must be willing to be led by grace, turning a blind eye to some things and a cheek to others—letting go of cynicism born of hurts and disappointments. In other words, we have to be forgiving. Dr. Emerson Eggerichs captured the power of forgiveness in a marriage relationship with just a few articulated words in his book *Love & Respect*, "When you forgive him for being unloving, you give up your right to hold a grudge and be disrespectful in return.

By forgiving, you gain strength and freedom, and, amazingly, in many instances you halt the Crazy Cycle." Words of wisdom? Absolutely! Do we need them? Without a doubt. Is this the advice we relish when our husbands have offended us to the core, when we feel that their very presence is offensive and we cannot stand one more moment of them? Probably not. We are flesh, and the Bible reminds us that our flesh is weak. This innate weakness often leads to strong words and unbending attitudes when marital conflicts arise. That is why Jesus Christ must be at the center of our marriages. He is the Master Teacher Who understands us and knows our struggles when it comes to forming a healthy, loving, and forgiving relationship with our husbands. When He is present, our weak flesh has a hiding place where it is tempered and brought under submission to the authority of God, our source of strength and very present help in time of need. I cannot imagine a marriage that never needs God's help, including my own. I hope I never forget when—in a moment of what is politely referred to as "intense fellowship"—a word of wisdom flashed through my brain. It said, "Kindness." It was as if the still, small voice of the Lord spoke into my thoughts, piercing through the ungodly things I was thinking and wanting to say. It was humbling. I felt ashamed. That simple, to-the-point correction in my spirit pulled me back from the edges of myself where my emotions are most raw.

What marriage does better than any other relationship is to take our attitudes to task. We never know when or how an excruciating test of our commitment will come, but it will surely come, and for many of us, it will come more often than we ever imagined. Such are the dark times of marriage, when the only thing we want to do is dump the whole thing—not in the recycling bin, but in the trash compactor. And yet, they are the times when we need to stop and ask ourselves some uncomfortable questions. Is our concept of marriage lining up with biblical principles? Are our frustrations, anger, and disappointments the only passions we feel for our husbands? Are we honoring our husbands with our attitudes and thoughts or secretly wishing we were free from them or that they were other men—men from our past or our imaginations? Are we looking outside our marriages for appreciation, affirmation, and significance, risking a fall (or actually falling) into adulterous relationships, or are we working to overcome our hurts, fears, and anger, so that they don't become foxholes in our marriages? Have we surrendered our emotions to the authority of Christ through prayer and sought His grace to revive our bride-perspectives so that we can see our husbands through loving, adoring eyes? Are we relating to them with kindness and praying for their welfare, for their heart's desires, and for the manifestation of God's plan for them in our marriages? Do we have enough faith and love to lug our marriages to Calvary and sink them into the solid ground that is cleansed for us with the blood of Jesus, trusting that He can resurrect what is dead? Yet, in all of that, we need to remember James 2:20, which reminds us that faith without works is useless.

My experience has taught me that works are harder than faith when it comes to attitudes and emotions. It's hard to contain the foxes once they've been stirred. In the early days of my marriage, my first response was to shut down—give Morris the silent treatment and refuse to talk to him for days. Once, he asked me, "How long are you going to be angry?" The truth is, my silence may have begun out of anger, but, ultimately, it was a failed effort to punish him, to manipulate his emotions and, in some absurd way, feel victorious. Even after years of working out oneness with him, there are still times when dealing with my little foxes is a challenge. My first response is to try pushing them back. When that doesn't work, I try to outsmart them with pleasant thoughts. My last response is the only one that works: accepting that I cannot manage them by myself, that I need the help of Jesus: His Power, His Truth, and His Presence.

There are practical things we can do to add to our faith as we press forward in Christ, doing the awesome work of oneness. We must be willing to admit that there is work to be done. All marriages have struggles that will not go away without honesty and mutual effort to make appropriate corrections. It is our responsibility (and our husbands') to develop ways of managing conflicts; otherwise, they become a way of life, unresolved, and deeply embedded into our subconscious attitudes toward one another. A common conflict in marriage is the inability to listen to one another. So often, we listen to the words swirling around in our heads instead of the ones being spoken, creating a cyclical pattern of misunderstandings. Years ago, Morris and I fell into that pattern, which made meaningful communication difficult if not impossible. Instead of acting in accordance with what one or the other actually said (especially as it related to feelings or concerns), we responded out of our respective interpretations of the words used, prompted by emotional triggers. To correct it, we booked a hotel room (a neutral environment) and took with us two legal-size pads and two pens. With these tools, we began a weekend marriage intervention. The rules were simple. We were to take turns writing out our particular frustrations on our individual pads and reading them to each other, one grievance at a time. Only the person reading could speak. If I were reading, Morris had to listen without interrupting, and vice versa. We could not argue or become defensive about what was being said. Our work was to hear and internalize. After each issue was read, the listener was to acknowledge what was said and offer a corrective response (stated and written) that was sincere, satisfactory, and respectful of what was said. Morris and I did this for hours. It was amazing how many topics we covered and resolved because we didn't just listen in a superficial way, we actually took the time to hear each other and quiet our own reflexive thoughts. It was an effective work of oneness that provided a record of commitment to being more sensitive to each other's needs and concerns, and to hear each other.

When we pledged to love our husbands for better or for worse, we made a promise to love them unconditionally. In doing so, we set a high bar for ourselves. This bar demands all the strength, determination, and faith in God we can muster. But with perseverance and a lot of humility, we are able to reach it and pull ourselves over it without tearing our arms out of their sockets. Jesus is our source for getting over the bar. It is in Him, living through us, that we find courage to carry on, to do the work, and humble ourselves enough to soften our edges when marriage gets tough. When we rely on Him, we are empowered through Him to activate His character within ourselves. We gain strength through Him to persevere, to go beyond our attitudes, opinions, and emotions, and revive our bride-perspectives, respect our husbands, and keep our promises to love them with an agape love, for better or for worse, regardless of how we feel. This is how we live marriage by *The Book*. When we do this— when we choose to do what is right in spite of how we feel at any given time—we are doing the awesome work of oneness; we are choosing to be the likeness of Christ. This is the message in Philippians 2:3–4, which says, "Let nothing be done through selfish ambition or conceit, but in lowliness of mind let each esteem others better than himself. Let each of you look out not only for his own interests, but also for the interests of others."

Working Out Oneness

How is your faith in God reflected by your love for your husband?

_____

What does 1 Corinthians 13:4–7 mean to you in your marriage relationship?

_____

What are your methods for building a strong and successful marriage?

_____

Have you received good Christian counseling prior to marrying or during marriage? If so, how has it benefited your marriage relationship?

_____

What surprised you about your husband's expectations of married life and of you?

_____

What are the little foxes in your marriage?

_____

Do you ever feel powerless in your marriage? If so, how? And how do you manage your emotions?

_____

Do you have regrets about your attitude and responses to unexpected or unwanted situations? What has been the cost to you and your marriage as a result of your attitudes or actions?

_____

How often do you go to God for help with your marriage challenges and surrender them to the authority of Christ?

_____

How do you view marriage in terms of a covenant with God and your husband?

_____

When married life feels like it is at its worst rather than at its best, how much do you reflect on the vows you made at your wedding and the love you felt when you were a bride?

_____

Would you say that your marriage is by The Book?

_____

For Richer or Poorer

*Not that I speak in regard to need, for I have
learned in whatever state I am, to be content*
(Philippians 4:11)

"I've been poor and I've been rich. Rich is better!" These are the words of Beatrice Kaufman, a New York City writer and editor of the 1930s, wife of playwright George S. Kaufman. What is most fascinating about her sentiment is the underlying message pointing to the ephemeral nature of riches: there is every chance that they will slip right through our fingers. The Bible raises it to an assurance in Proverbs 23:4–5, "Do not overwork to be rich; because of your own understanding, cease! Will you set your eyes on that which is not: For riches certainly make themselves wings; they fly away like an eagle toward heaven." They fly away for any number of reasons: living too high, job loss, illness, catastrophic events, or poor money management. But who is thinking of such things when wedding bells are ringing? We are in love and excited about the future with our brand new husbands, and we have promised to love them whether we are rich or poor.

What happens when that promise comes under attack because of money problems: when there is no money to pay off our credit card debt, no money to pay the household bills, no money to stock our pantries or prevent the banks from repossessing our homes or cars? Much has been studied and written about the stress that failed finances impose on marriages. One such study, "Examining the Relationship Between Financial Issues and Divorce," by Jeffrey Dew, Sonya Britt, and Sandra Houston suggests that "financial disagreements are stronger predictors of divorce relative to other common marital disagreements." It would seem that Beatrice Kaufman is right: Richer is better. Indeed, it is true that richer feels better than poorer, and it is also true that riches are hard to give up; for some of us, it is impossible. Jesus illustrates this in the parable about the rich young man.

> Now as He (Jesus) was going out on the road, one came running, knelt before Him, and asked Him, "Good Teacher, what shall I do that I may inherit eternal life?" Then Jesus, looking at him, loved him, and said to him, "One thing you lack: Go your way, sell whatever you have and give to the poor, and you will have treasure in heaven; and come, take up the cross, and follow Me."

> But he was sad at this word, and went away sorrowful, for he had great possessions. Then Jesus looked around and said to His disciples, "How hard it is for those who have riches to enter the Kingdom of God!"

> The disciples were astonished at His words. But Jesus answered again and said to them, "Children, how hard it is for those who trust in riches to enter the Kingdom of God!" (Mark 10:17, 21–24)

This story always makes me think of Jesus when He was in Caesarea, Philippi, speaking to the disciples and the townspeople saying, "For what will it profit a man if he gains the whole world, and loses his soul?" (Mark 8:36) What is tragic about this man is that he made a conscious decision to choose death over life, temporal riches over eternal treasures. We would not intentionally trade our souls for riches. We just don't want to be poor. We want the good life. We want the advantages of affluence. We want them for ourselves, our husbands, and our children. It's called success; and success, from a cultural perspective, is measured by riches: how much money we make, what kind of cars we drive, where we live, where our children attend school, where we shop, and what labels are sewn into our clothing. But where does *want* end and *avarice* begin? This dilemma is not limited to the secular world. Churches all around the country are replete with ostentation, from the pastors to the congregants. Yet, riches are a blessing from God, intended to glorify Him. Jesus wants us to prosper. It is greed and the tendency to put our trust in riches that compromise our godly perspectives and, thus, our marriage relationships. Unwittingly, we create our own stumbling blocks to righteous living and a spirit of contentment. Jesus says, "Do not store up for yourselves treasures on earth, where moths and vermin destroy, and where thieves break in and steal. But store up for yourselves treasures in heaven, where moths and vermin do not destroy, and where thieves do not break in and steal. For where your treasure is, there your heart will be also." (Matthew 6:19–21 NIV)

This is the moment of truth when we must ask ourselves: Where is our treasure? Is it in the vows we took to love whether rich or poor? Is it in our faith in God? Is it in His promise to deliver the righteous from all afflictions? (Psalm 34:19) Where do we stand when it comes to money? What is our response when a financial crisis embattles our marriages? If we treasure money and things more than we love our husbands, not only do we not love our husbands as we promised, we don't love God as we should. He is the One who "makes poor and makes rich; He brings low and lifts up. He raises the poor from the dust and lifts the beggar from the ash heap, to set them among princes and make them inherit the throne of glory." (1 Samuel 2:7) He holds the answer to our money woes in the palm of His hand, for He is our ultimate provider; He owns the silver and the gold. (Haggai 2:8) Our job, in times of financial stress, is to turn to Jesus in faith and, through Him, seek the Kingdom of God and His righteousness first; trusting that as we surrender to Him, everything else will be added, in accordance with the truth of His Word. (Matthew 6:33)

But let's be clear. That kind of faith is not an acquiescence requiring no effort on our part. We have a responsibility to couple our trust in God with initiative, by putting our gifts and talents to work to help our husbands, including generating income when needed, and being good stewards over our finances, whether great or small. What's more, Romans 13:8 says that we are to "let no debt remain." It is one thing for us to learn—as did the apostle Paul—to be content in whatever state we find ourselves. It is another thing to create a state of lack by being wasteful or unwise with our finances, blithely believing that God will restore what we have squandered. Equally ungodly is selfish behavior from husbands who control the purse strings with an iron grip and micromanage our wants and needs, leaving us to feel impoverished and unloved. We are to honor God with our wealth. (Proverbs 3:9 NIV) That means we are to be grateful, prudent, and generous with whatever we have. Anything else, in the context of marriage, is a recipe for strife and, in many instances, divorce. There is a verse in the Book of Proverbs that ministers to my heart when I am facing the hard stuff of marriage (including the challenges of money) and have lost all semblance of a bride-perspective. I remember what a godsend it was to me when Morris and I struggled through a torturous financial collapse. At the time, our life together was measured by the distance between bad news and broken dreams. It seemed that even if I squinted, I couldn't see a glimmer of light shining from the end of our tunnel. I felt frustrated and, I must admit, sometimes tempted to cut and run. It was difficult for me to resist my impulse to rage against the darkness. My saving grace was the verse. It was my refuge, but more than that, it was my witness to the promise I had made when I was a bride: to love for richer or poorer. That verse says, "A wise woman builds her home, but a foolish woman tears it down with her own hands. (14:1 NLT) Though I was tired of the tension between us and the constant stress of too many months and too little money, in my heart, I did not want to tear down my home or discard my marriage. I was no longer the immature, young wife I was many years before, when I complained to my mother that I had made a mistake in getting married, to which she responded, "You will have to go home and fix your mistake." What I wanted was relief from the struggle; I wanted to get back to the place of comfort. Up to that point, it had never occurred to me that our living standard could change so dramatically that we would not have plenty of money at our disposal to use in whatever way pleased us. We had always had more than enough, even when we were first married living in a three-room apartment. God had been good to us, and we prospered. We had lovely homes, a savings account, up-to-date cars, private schooling for our children, summer vacations, timeshare properties—we didn't want for anything. And because the shift was gradual, I believed that we would soon change course and begin an ascent, rather like an airplane that loses altitude and suddenly starts to lift, its nose pointing upwards, pulling itself toward the heavens. That didn't happen. The plunge was frightening. But God held the yoke that determined our direction. It was because of His great love that we did not crash and burn. We stabilized and continued on a fresh wind, somewhere between trust, faith, and work.

The trouble with money is that, while it is the source by which we acquire our comforts, it is unpredictable and vulnerable to external events. Just like an airplane, it can take you to great heights; but confronted with unexpected or unfavorable conditions, it can disappear from the radar screen. Whether or not a financial blackout wrecks our marriages depends on where our treasures lie. Comfort is great, contentment is better. Contentment is not constrained by our desires. It is open-ended, which allows Jesus to enter into our circumstances at any time, from any point, and work the wonders of His will. He has a plan for our lives which may not look at all like our plans for ourselves. His thoughts are not our thoughts, neither are His ways our ways. (Isaiah 55:8) The harder we pursue our comforts, the farther we go from God. Jesus said in Luke 12:15, "Take heed and beware of covetousness, for one's life does not consist in the abundance of the things he possesses." When we seek contentment, inevitably, we draw closer to God because contentment brings peace. God is our peace. Therefore, we are to be anxious for nothing, but in everything by prayer and supplication, with thanksgiving, let our requests be made known to God; and His peace, which surpasses all understanding, will guard our hearts and minds through Christ Jesus. (Philippians 4:6–7

Why is it that, so often, those words are insufficient to allay our fears of not having enough? My guess is that in a material world (which is what we live in), the temptation to pursue comfort, to shop, to eat out, and to be entertained is overpowering. The momentary pleasures of comfort captivate us just as surely as the persuasive guile of Satan charmed Eve. We need the peace of God to guard our hearts and minds because, without His peace, we are bound by our desires and fears, which oppose contentment.

Though we may not admit it (and perhaps don't realize it), when we choose comfort over contentment, we place our hope in our money and we make ourselves vulnerable to the deceit of money. The result is a spiritual heart condition brought on by a clot in our faith. As long as that clot remains, we cannot breathe freely. We feel stifled, frustrated, hurt, and betrayed because our money has taken a dive, making the comforts we love and want unobtainable. In his story *Perelandra*, C. S. Lewis writes, "This itch to have things over again, as if life were a film that could be unrolled twice or even made to work backwards ... was it possibly the root of all evil? No, of course the love of money was called that. But money itself—perhaps one valued it chiefly as a defense against chance, a security for being able to have things over again, a means of arresting the unrolling of the film." We need money. But how much is enough for us to be content? What price are we willing to pay to have more? Is it the price of our families, our integrity, our humanity, our peace—our promises to God and our husbands? In 1945, Warner Brothers released the film *Mildred Pierce*. It is one of my favorite films because it is a wonderful illustration of 1 Timothy 6:9: "Those who want to get rich fall into temptation and a trap and into many foolish and harmful desires that plunge people into ruin and destruction." (NIV) The story of *Mildred Pierce* is about discontent and disillusion born out of the desire for more—more than the Pierce family had in their till. The opening scene begins with Mildred working in the kitchen baking pies and cakes to sell to her neighborhood customers. Like most married women of her era, she was a homemaker. However, her husband, Bert, was out of work, having lost his partnership status with a real estate firm. Mildred's focus was on earning income to fill the gap while Bert sought employment. It appeared that Mildred and Bert, along with their two daughters, Veda and Kay, had enjoyed a middle-class lifestyle until the money disappeared.

With tensions high, Mildred and Bert got into a heated argument which ended with the two agreeing to separate. Eventually, Mildred opened a restaurant, and then another and another until she had a chain of successful restaurants operating. She was smart, with a business savvy that made her a natural for entrepreneurship. Through hard work and determination, she built a lucrative enterprise, netting enough money for every conceivable extravagance; and she indulged herself and her daughters, regularly, especially Veda. But what followed her excesses were temptations, traps, and many foolish and harmful desires that led to the destruction of the family. In the end, the money that Mildred pursued in order to join the ranks of the wealthy became a road to perdition, where her hopes and dreams fell to ruin. With everything gone: the dissolution of her restaurants, one daughter deceased and the other imprisoned, she reunited with Bert—a life without riches, but a life rich in contentment.

Although *Mildred Pierce* is about a fictitious wife who was overwrought from financial stress, it illustrates some of the pitfalls awaiting us when we set out on a circuitous journey out of the will of God to achieve our goals. Mildred sought a better life by dispensing with her marriage, her home, and her discretion in order to acquire on her own what her husband could not provide. Though her actions might have been preemptive, her expectation of her husband to be the primary provider was normal. Dr. Emmerson Eggerichs, speaking about his assessment of the typical woman writes in his book *Love and Respect*: "As she evaluates her future with a man, she instinctively considers his ability to take care of her and the children. The good-willed woman marries for love, not for money; nonetheless, she is very aware of the need to make a `nest.'" Taking a somewhat different angle in *His Needs, Her Needs,* Willard F. Harley, Jr., writes: "In truth a woman does marry a man for his money ... Most wives do not only expect their husbands to work, they also expect them to earn enough to support their families." When circumstances interrupt the normal flow of income, creating a protracted financial crisis that threatens the "nest," worry ensues; tempers fly. Even when our marriages are strong, there is a pernicious coolness that seeps into our hearts when money becomes our main focus and source of worry. It weakens oneness by draining trust from our marriages. We don't feel secure, therefore, we worry, which breeds distrust. When trust is gone, respect goes with it. Little by little, those warm, loving feelings that gushed out of us when we were brides, suffocate under the weight of frayed emotions.

So how do we avoid becoming a Mildred when a money crisis confronts our presumptions of security? Jesus said in Matthew 6:25–26, "Therefore I say to you, do not worry about your life, what you will eat or what you will drink; nor about your body, what you will put on. Is not life more than food and the body more than clothing? Look at the birds of the air, for they neither sow nor reap nor gather into barns; yet your heavenly Father feeds them. Are you not of more value than they?" In a material world, this tender advice, though heartening, is tough to follow. It is hard not to worry when we are faced with the possibility of losing our homes or do not have decent food or clothing for ourselves or our children.

But here's the problem with worry. It doesn't alter our situations nor does it lessen our fears about our situations. In fact, worry can do nothing to calm our fears because worry, itself, is a form of fear. When we are fearful, we are more prone to making mistakes. We are vulnerable to acts of desperation and missed opportunities, since fear obscures clarity. We need to remember—especially when times are tough—that worry and fear are not of God. They are the works of the devil, to steal our peace. God must be our guiding force whether we are rich or poor. He is the One Who opens doors that no one can shut and straightens our crooked paths. (Revelation 3:8; Isaiah 45:2) He, and only He, knows the plans He has to prosper us; and His plans are not to harm us, but to give us hope and a future. (Jeremiah 29:11) Yes, we should be aspirational and excited about using our gifts and talents for the betterment of ourselves and our families. And, yes, we should pursue our careers and employment opportunities. But we must be careful not to put our ambitions above our families. Our professional and personal goals should never become a destructive force in our homes but rather an asset—a blessing, helping to uphold the strength and welfare of the family and household. We should be inspirational as well—a shining example of encouragement to and appreciation of our husbands and children, in good and bad times. This is God's desire for us. Every time we connect with His desires for our lives, we invite Him into our homes, our marriages, and our children's lives, where He can work to will and to act in order to fulfill His good purpose. (Philippians 2:13)

What, then, is the takeaway for our money challenges with respect to the Mildred effect? It is that she is a reflection of the Eve in us—our penchant to pursue what *we* want, what *we* think is best, and what *we* believe will empower us and make us feel secure. She is a reminder that we must seek God first and allow Him to lead us. God wants us to prosper in life, but by *The Book*, within the context of His will. He knows what we lack and what we need. But He is a God of order, and His order is tied to His will. In marriage, as in all things, He is the first order of business. He wants us to take Him at His word and seek His Kingdom and His righteousness before we do anything else; then all the rest will be added. This is how His order works; this is how we get through the dark times with our faith and our marriages intact. It is not an easy course to follow because it pushes us to the frontiers of our faith where we must wait on Him, and waiting is the hardest part. I can speak for myself and say that I don't like waiting. It requires that virtue which I have in short supply: patience. However, I am convinced that when we do it alone—when pursuing our God-given dreams bypasses God (the Source of our dreams) and turns into striving for more and more material comfort at any cost, we miss the mark, we miss our purpose, and we miss God. Jesus repeats His admonition in Matthew 6: 30–33 (NASB):

> *You of little faith! Do not worry then, saying, "What will we eat?" or "What will we drink?" or "What will we wear for clothing?" For the Gentiles eagerly seek all these things; for your heavenly Father knows that you need all these things. But seek first His kingdom and His righteousness, and all these things will be added to you.*

Jesus is telling us in the clearest of words to let go of striving for material comforts and trust Him to meet our needs. That is where we find peace. It is how we unburden ourselves and make room for God's plan for our prosperity to manifest in our lives. It is the place where we relinquish our fears so that we can experience joy again in our marriage relationships, and rediscover the oneness we shared with our husbands when our love was fresh and we were content, before there was strife, when we were their brides.

Working Out Oneness

What does Matthew 6:12 mean to you with respect to your marriage?

_____

What is your first reaction when money's too tight: worry, fear, anger, frustration, patience, prayer, or trust in the Lord?

_____

How do you view God's role in your life when you feel financially threatened?

_____

How responsible are you with money management? What are your boundaries for living within your means? How is that working for you?

_____

How do you relate to Proverbs 14:1? Are you a wise woman, or are you tearing down your home with your own hands?

———————————————————————————————

Do you spend more time and energy seeking comfort or contentment? How is your preference affecting your marriage relationship?

———————————————————————————————

When it comes to managing money, are you and your husband in agreement?

———————————————————————————————

Does the lack of financial stability cause you to take drastic steps, or does it draw you closer to your husband?

———————————————————————————————

What is your view regarding the financial obligation for marriage? Do you believe that husbands are the primary breadwinner and should earn enough money to support the family, or do you think it is the obligation of wives as well?

_____

How does oneness factor into the financial responsibilities inherent in marriage?

_____

In what ways are you making room for God to work in your life and to prosper you according to His plan?

_____

In Sickness and in Health

Beloved, I pray that you may prosper in all things
and be in health, just as your soul prospers.
(3 John 1:2)

There is a reason that the apostle John wrote, "Beloved, I pray that you may prosper in all things and be in health, just as your soul prospers." John understood that without health, it is difficult to press on toward the purposes of God. So he is fervent in wanting all who are in Christ to serve in good health. Marriage is a service unto the LORD, created by Him to glorify Him, even if modern culture suggests otherwise. Marriage is work, and like any work, it is easier when we are in good health. We see that played out during Job's sickness and in the manner in which his wife responded to him. Sickness comes to us all. In marriage, one spouse or the other will become a caretaker at some point. Nowhere is the evidence of that fact more clear than in the heart-wrenching details presented in Job 2:7–8. We know that his situation was bad; and we know it was the source of great distress for him and his wife. But there are three important lessons we can take from their story. Serious illness can challenge us in ways we never thought possible. Caring for a loved one through catastrophic illness can be exhausting, both emotionally and physically, making us vulnerable to insensitivities toward the ones we love the most in the world. We can become shallow, forgetting those opening words in 1 Corinthians 13:4, *love is patient, love is kind,* and fall backwards into the selfish side of our natures.

Acts of love, patience, and kindness for others during seasons of illness are not specific to wives who become caretakers. They apply to husbands who find themselves in that role as well. Kathy Collard Miller and D. Larry Miller, co-authors of *What's in the Bible for Couples,* assert that, "Regardless of the difficulty, it is up to us to accept the circumstances and our spouses. If we are being shallow in marriage, shallowness could be expressed as selfishness, anger, or unfaithfulness."

Words like *shallowness, selfishness,* and *anger* should be as unwelcome in married life as a thief is in our homes. Thieves steal what is precious, what is valuable, what we cherish. Harsh words and heartless attitudes do the same thing in our marriages. They ravage our relationships. Yet I will venture to say that every married couple is guilty of expressing this kind of raw emotion, even Christian couples, when circumstances become hard, persistent, and seemingly unmanageable. I have done it and wished I could swallow my tongue. When Job's wife spewed those ugly words while he was in agony and at his lowest, she was shallow, selfish, and angry. But we know that she was overwhelmed and, most likely, at her wits' end.

> *For though we walk in the flesh, we do not war according to the flesh. For the weapons of our warfare are not carnal but mighty in God for pulling down strongholds, casting down arguments and every high thing that exalts itself against the knowledge of God, bringing every thought into captivity to the obedience of Christ... . (2 Corinthians 10:3–5)*

All of us are limited in what we can handle without losing composure. Jesus said, "Come to Me, all you who labor and are heavy laden, and I will give you rest." (Matthew 11:28) We need to reach out to Him for the help He offers, so that we can respond to our challenges appropriately with mercy, grace, and a humble spirit. We need to tap into Hebrews 4:16 "and come boldly to the throne of grace, that we may obtain mercy and find grace to help in time of need." Just think how differently Job's wife might have responded had she reached out to the LORD before speaking. There is wisdom to be had, always, from the Word of God. Job understood that and relied on God's Word. Remember when Eliphaz (one of Job's dubious friends) likened Job to a foolish man and a simpleton? Job did not return insult for insult. He said, "Anyone who withholds kindness from a friend forsakes the fear of the Almighty." (Job 6:14 NIV) Suppose his wife had taken a cue from his response to Eliphaz and applied that message to herself? Had she done so, she might have restrained her tongue and sought the LORD for help and grace, even listened for His voice, quietly coaxing her into His peace—His calming stillness. In silence, she might have articulated the poetic counsel offered in Mrs. Charles E. Cowman's book, *Streams in the Desert*:

> "Be still! Just be still!
> There comes a presence very mild and sweet;
> White are the sandals of His noiseless feet.
> It is the Comforter whom Jesus sent
> To teach thee what the words He uttered meant.
> The willing, waiting spirit, He doth fill.
> If thou would'st hear His message,
> Dear soul, be still!"

If she had stopped and listened, perhaps she would have thought twice about withholding kindness from Job when he needed it so desperately. Maybe she would have shown him compassion during his bout with boils and offered words of comfort, a salve for his affliction, warm baths to soothe the horrendous itching and pain that accompanied his boils. But because she was controlled by her emotions, her own grief and suffering rather than the Spirit of Grace, she could offer him nothing except harsh condemnation.

The story of Job gives lengthy details of his anguish, nothing of hers. But it doesn't take much imagination to understand that she was devastated in the most excruciating sense of the word. And who knows what it was like for her, in the midst of her suffering, to hear Job complaining about why this terrible thing had happened to *him*, or listen to his arguments with his so-called friends about the reason for *his* situation, or even his debate with God about why He had allowed such disaster to befall *him*, not to mention his long laments about why he was born.

> *"Why did I not die at birth? Why did I not perish when I came from the womb? Why did the knees receive me? Or why the breasts, that I should nurse? For now I would have lain still and been quiet. I would have been asleep; then I would have been at rest with kings and counselors of the earth, who built ruins for themselves, or with princes who had gold, who filled their houses with silver; or why was I not hidden like a stillborn child, like infants who never saw light?" (Job 3:11–16)*

Maybe she was sick and tired of listening to his grumblings of self-pity, given the fact that she was in agony, too. At least

Job's so-called friends showed up for a shiva visit. Where were his wife's friends? Where were her BFFs—the ones who could share in her grief and console her with their very presence, a hug, a word of encouragement, at minimum, a covered dish?

Nonetheless, her response was not out of her grief alone. It was fueled by bitterness, fear, and anger at the sudden loss of her children and the shift from riches to rags, blessings to curses, and an uncertain future. This aberrational descent into utter deprivation had to be unimaginable to her, and it was not limited to the loss of her family and material goods; she lost her spiritual footing as well. She did not have Hebrews 10:35–37 to caution her: "So do not throw away your confidence; it will be richly rewarded. You need to persevere so that when you have done the will of God, you will receive what He has promised. For, in just a little while, He Who is coming will come and will not delay." (NIV) With her faith shattered and her heart broken, she could not persevere through the added stress of Job's hideous disease. The disaster that swept through their marriage should have brought them closer together, causing them to cling to one another for solace, survival, and whatever remnants of life and love remained. Instead, there was distance. Job was dismayed and she was despairing. Most likely, both she and Job had enjoyed good health. She never could have dreamed that Satan would gain permission from God to kill, steal, and destroy her family, her home, and Job's health. When the whirlwind came, her faith and trust in God were blown away along with everything else, making the way for bitterness and anger to fill the void in her soul. Forget bride-memories! Her deep sorrow had smothered any gentleness her spirit once held and suffocated her ability to persevere lovingly with Job. Yet, her responsibility—her obligation to her covenant to care for him and love him in sickness and in health—remained.

What was true for her is true for us. We are responsible for working through the hard stuff and upholding our covenant, not only for ourselves, but for the encouragement of others—fellow wives who are struggling in their marriages and feel disheartened, women who wish to be married but are leery of the work, and women who are about to be married and are inspired by our testimonies—that our marriages are instruments of God, designed by Him for us, and for His glory. Yet, it is also true that lingering illness can (and often does) create severe stress in our marriages, throwing us off balance emotionally, physically, and spiritually. But God has given us the power of self-control through His Spirit and His Word. We can follow the teaching of the apostle Paul, in 1 Corinthians 9:27, and discipline ourselves by bringing our emotions into subjection and obedience to God, through Jesus Christ. When we do that, we have reinforcement; and a cord of three strands is not quickly broken. (Ecclesiastes 4:12) With Him at the center, that same stress is transformed into the very confidence we need to move forward in our marriages. Then we are able to reset our focus, because we have an advocate and protector sustaining us, and a source of strength when we are weak.

That was Emmet's perspective when Candice called him and told him that the lump in her breast tested positive for cancer. His calm, optimistic, and prayerful attitude was the exact comfort she needed, as she struggled with the word *malignant*, dogging her every thought.

> *I was in shock! I couldn't believe that this was happening to me. I knew that I had a lump. I found it two years before my cancer diagnosis. A biopsy was done at that time, and I was told that the lump was not cancerous.*

With that assurance, she went on with her life, attending to her home, the three children, and her husband, Emmet. A year and a half went by before she scheduled her next mammogram.

> *I always went for my regular, yearly exam, but this time I put it off. When I went for my check-up, they told me that something was there and that they wanted to biopsy the area. The doctor let me know that he was concerned and that he would get back to me with the test results.*

When the test results came back confirming the doctor's fears, Candice had a lot of questions: *What am I going to do now? What does all this mean?* She wanted Emmet to know her every thought, to ask her questions about what was happening, and to give her answers regarding the horrific invasion taking place in her body. But he didn't ask questions, he listened to her, prayed with her, and comforted her.

> *He didn't have answers. He had never had breast cancer, and he didn't want to tell me how I should feel.*

Candice and Emmet were at the crest of one those clarifying moments that take the measure of a marriage. The vows they had exchanged to love each other in sickness and in health were suddenly central to their relationship and would remain so for many months to come. Candice was experiencing the worst kind of anguish, second only to the pain she felt when she delivered her stillborn infant, a little boy, nineteen years earlier. Now, she was undergoing the loss of her left breast.

Seeing myself right after surgery was devastating. I'll be honest. I was not happy about that. I was angry, sad, and surprised! But the hospital staff was very encouraging. They told me the process of getting back to normal was a marathon and that they would do everything to get me back to a place of comfort. Emmet was a big part of my healing. He was my caretaker. He helped me keep a right perspective about trusting God and staying focused on Him. He went to all the treatment appointments with me, and after the surgery, he emptied the drainage tubes, took my temperature, and recorded all the different things we needed for my postsurgery visits. He tried to make things easier by preparing my meals, caring for the children, getting them to their activities, organizing the house—he did all this while managing a full time job. It was draining.

There were times, though, despite Emmet's loving care, when it annoyed Candice that he never seemed to listen when she tried to share the details about her cancer.

Sometimes I would want to discuss what the doctor said. Or, if I got fearful because of something I read or heard, he wouldn't want to talk about it. That bothered me. But I wasn't perfect. I would equate his attitude to not caring, and that would hurt his feelings. He would say, "I don't understand why you think that I don't care after all I am doing and will continue to do? I cannot always meet your

expectations!" Maybe, sometimes, my expectations
were too high.

Maybe it was about differences. Candice's need to discuss every detail of her cancer and treatments was internally driven by her profound sense of vulnerability. She was the one who was experiencing trauma to her body and mind. Emmet, on the other hand, experienced her need to share her concerns from an external perspective, as a witness and respondent. What's more, he is project manager, by profession, accustomed to processing information in a hierarchical fashion: important versus urgent. It is possible, and very likely, that he is more pragmatic than perceptive. It is also possible that he wanted to keep his spiritual ears clear for hearing the still, small voice of the Lord guiding him, strengthening him, and preparing him for the challenges ahead.

Candice's treatments were taxing. She endured pain resulting from the mastectomy (and of feeling mutilated), sickness and fatigue due to chemotherapy and radiation, and later, myriad discomforts from multiple procedures to reconstruct her breast. Being a man of deep faith, who holds a Master of Divinity degree, Emmet remained focused on the big picture, on moving forward by *The Book*, keeping his eyes on Jesus. He might have felt it crucial to remain positive, free from anxiety fueled by too much information. He was keenly aware that the devil prowls around like a roaring lion, looking for someone he can devour. (1 Peter 5:8) Perhaps, for Emmet, managing his emotions by staying alert and of sober mind was of greater importance than the urgency of a given moment. He had to stay centered. How could he have encouraged Candice as he did, day after day, month after month, through each grueling treatment, if he had not understood, according to the grace given him, that there is a time to speak and a time to keep silent? More important, how could he have inspired her in the face of it all, to hold fast to her faith in God—to trust His plans to prosper her and not harm her, to give her hope and a future—if he had become unnerved by taking in more information than he could manage— details over which he had no control? He believed the promise of God: that nothing was too difficult for Him. (Jeremiah 29:11, 32: 27 NIV) Emmet's confidence was in the name that is above all names, Jesus Christ, and the skill of the doctors He provided to manage Candice's cancer treatments and outcome.

> I would not have gotten through this without Emmet. I am so grateful for his faith, his knowledge of God, and his ability to share it.

Her gratitude for his strength of faith is not to suggest that her own faith was lacking; rather, it is an indicator that her faith was being tested in a mortal way and needed infusions of hope, much like the body needs more fluids when exposed to scorching temperatures. Candice was fighting for her life. She was young. She had a family—children who needed her, and her body and soul were under attack. Who among us is not shaken when adversity strikes? All of us are in the boat with Peter when it comes to rising up in faith. We want to believe that we can step out onto the night waters that surround us with our eyes fixed on Jesus. But let a storm come with blustery winds and rising waves crashing against our worst fears and we see how quickly we sink, how much more of Jesus we need to buttress our faith. Sickness can be that kind of storm pounding against our marriages, our minds, stirring up our insecurities and dampening our resolve with the spirit of Job's wife. But the Bible tells us that we do not have to sink, because we have a High Priest Who is able to sympathize with our weaknesses, Who was tempted as we are, yet without sin. Therefore, we can come boldly to the Throne of Grace and receive mercy and grace sufficient to help us when we need it most. (Hebrews 4:15–16) In the end, it's about love: God's love for us and our love for each other, no matter what the night brings.

> *The easy way out is to run from something that's hard to deal with. But that's not what you do in a marriage. The commitment is to God, so if sickness comes, He sees it, and He knows how to give us what we need to sustain us through it. But it's a hard one for marriage. You fall in love with a person that is one way; if that person changes because of sickness and is no longer the same, do you throw away the marriage? No, you don't. You continue to love that person, in sickness and in health.*

Working Out Oneness

Have you ever had to care for your husband through bouts of illness? How did you manage the demands on your time? Was the experience a drain on your emotions? If so, how?

When we live marriage by The Book, we are aligned with 1 Corinthians 13:4 in matters of sickness and health. How successful are you at responding according to that biblical edict?

What do you think was missing from Job's wife's sense of oneness?

When has Matthew 11:28 rescued you from yourself because you lost control of your emotions?

How often do you stop to remember the covenant you made to love, when you were a bride, even when loving is exhausting?

Has illness ever brought such severe stress in your marriage that you felt off balance and insensitive to those you love?

Do you regard health matters as urgent or important?

Was there ever a time when illness became a thief stealing your faith in God? If so, what did you do to get back to trusting God and living by The Book?

What does Hebrews 4:15–16 mean to you?

Are you inclined to run from health challenges or take them to the Throne of Grace and put them in the hands of Jesus?

Are you an encourager in times of illness, when the journey to wellness is hard, or are you more like Job's wife, angry that life has presented you with this difficulty?

Till Death Do Us Part

And I will betroth you to me forever.
I will betroth you to me in righteousness and in
justice, in steadfast love and in mercy.
(Hosea 2:19)

God was not mincing words when He declared that we are one flesh with our husbands. And like a parent driving a point to dull-eared children, He repeated His edict in no uncertain terms: "So they are no longer two, but one flesh. Therefore what God has joined together, let no one separate." (Matthew 19: 5–6 NIV) How much clearer could it be? We are permanently bonded to our husbands and they to us, as if conjoined by the Word of God—intertwined and interdependent, our bodies no longer our own but each other's. This oneness—this covenantal coupling ordained by God is intended to endure, never breaking except by force of death.

All the same, it is impossible to talk about God's plan for lasting marriages without discussing the sabotaging effect of divorce. Put another way: Suppose we are at a track meet watching a runner racing toward the finish line and on the track is a final hurdle to be cleared. But instead of clearing it, the runner is entangled by it and brought crashing to the ground. Hurt and humiliated, the runner doesn't get up and push toward the finish line but rather accepts defeat and limps off the track. In a manner of speaking, we start out in a mad love dash, committed and focused—determined to give our marriages all we've got, so that we can run the course to the finish line just as we vowed to do when we were brides. But we give up. We give up largely because we live in a world of many tracks and high hurdles, where the concept of marriage is malleable, and where society teaches that marriage is good and worth the effort as long as it doesn't trip us up and cause hurt or humiliation. Jesus lived in our world. Imagine if He had quit on us when He was hurt and humiliated as a result of being entangled with us?

Divorce statistics suggest that the pledges we make when we stand at the altar and vow to love and cherish our husbands for better or worse, for richer or poorer, in sickness and in health—*till death do us part*, too often, are more ceremonial than serious. It's not that we are not intentional when we make those vows. The problem has to do with the various ways we view marriage, the men we choose, or our maturity for marriage. We spend thousands of dollars on wedding gowns, invitations, and flowers to get married, and thousands more on opulent venues for celebrating our nuptials. And why not? Why shouldn't our weddings be gloriously celebrated, if it is what we want and can afford? But, marriage! That's a different matter. Marriage is not about pageantry. It is about honoring our vows to each other and to God, understanding that there is no perfection in love except in Jesus Christ. C. S. Lewis offers a more somber sentiment saying, "To love at all is to be vulnerable. Love anything, and your heart will certainly be wrung and possibly be broken. If you want to make sure of keeping it intact, you must give your heart to no one, not even an animal. Wrap it carefully round with hobbies and little luxuries; avoid all entanglements; lock it up safe in the casket or coffin of your selfishness. But in that casket—safe, dark, motionless, airless—it will change. It will not be broken; it will become unbreakable, impenetrable, irredeemable."

This is where I pause to repeat myself: Marriage requires oneness, and oneness requires love. However, oneness, by its very nature is vulnerable to everything marriage has to offer: good and bad, because it is infected with humanness. Yet, it is in oneness that we find safety in love and marriage for a lifetime. This kind of safety—this kind of love—must be under submission to the obedience of Jesus Christ. That is the safe place where we are able to work out our differences together, in oneness, because we have the Spirit of the Lord working through us to temper our vulnerabilities, our human imperfections. If we are to make our marriages last to the end of our lives, *till death do us part*, we must have Jesus in the midst, perfecting our love and providing the strength, wisdom, and perseverance needed to overcome our foibles and frailties so that our love will not grow dark, motionless, and airless. But if that should happen and there is nothing left but shattered dreams, wedding photos, and films—all the lifeless memories of the way we were—it is our hearts that carry the burden and the scars. It is a sad and painful thing when so much love, anticipation, and investment turns to grief instead of forever. But more about that later.

For most of us, loving someone for the rest of our lives, working through the rough spots, building a family, and exploring life with him is basic to our natures and worthy of marriage. We see that manifested in how frequently we marry again, following divorce or death. Perhaps we do it because we are Adam's rib, instinctively seeking the missing part from which we came. What is certain is that it is easier to make a vow during the marriage ceremony than to keep one. We are not Stepford wives vacant and devoid of self-awareness, in mindless agreement with every word our husbands speak. Nor is marriage a haven of fair play, where everything is equal. No, marriage is give-and-take, but mostly give. It is choosing to love through the challenges of a shared life and being willing to forgive up to seventy times seven, until death parts us. (Matthew 18:21–22) It is a daily commitment to doing the awesome work of oneness. That's why marriage is hard work, if we are going to do it by *The Book*, honoring our vows and remaining married until we are separated by death. But for all our hard work, there are rewards. We have a lifetime of loving and being loved; we create legacy through the children we bear; and, by our obedience in upholding our vows, we glorify God, which is our ultimate purpose in being. And, of course, there is the joy of growing old together, which reminds me of a story I read about an elderly couple.

> *An eighty-year old couple was worried because they kept forgetting things all the time. The doctor assured them there was nothing seriously wrong except old age, and suggested they carry a notebook and write things down so they wouldn't forget. Several days later, the old man got up to go to the kitchen. His wife said, "Dear, get me a bowl of ice cream while you're up."*
>
> *"Ok," he said.*
> *His wife continued, "...and put some chocolate syrup on it—better write all this down."*
> *"I won't forget," he said. Twenty minutes later he came back into the room and handed her a plate of scrambled eggs and bacon.*
> *She glared at him. "Now, I told you to write it down! I knew you'd forget."*

"What did I forget?" he asked.
She replied, "My toast!"

In a youth-oriented society like ours, the idea of growing old together is a reminder of the unmerciful ravaging of time rather than the sweetness of maturing through oneness. But in fact, growing old together is, and should be, the fulfillment of God's plan for marriage to endure through our lifetimes. God never promised us a trouble-free marriage. But He promised to be our refuge, strength, and help in the midst of our troubles. (Psalm 46:1) It's just that we don't want troubles and don't anticipate them, not in a serious way, and not when we are brides.

Callie never imagined that her marriage to Nick would be one of the greatest challenges of her life, and that her efforts to honor her vow to be with him until death took him (or her) would turn her into a nervous wreck. She had dated him throughout her college years and admits there were rough spots in those days: several breakups and makeups, but she was inescapably drawn to him. She enjoyed being with him and loved his obvious confidence, of which she had none. They were opposite in every way, like two batteries in a flashlight: one positive, one negative, both trying to spark light into their relationship. The problem was that they were draining each other.

> *Immediately there was conflict. I was so insecure and idealistic. Back then, I was churched; I wasn't spiritual. I didn't see things through God's eyes. I had this view that marriage was going to be sweet and that Nick was just going to love me; we would be so happy. I was so stupid! I knew zero about relationships. I was in love with love. I think I was really looking for a daddy—somebody to be that*

man who would love me and cherish me, because my dad never did—not openly. He was a good man, a godly man, but he didn't know how to do that. I thought Nick was going to be that man, but he wasn't. He really loved me, but my expectations of him were unrealistic. That's why I was in shock after we married.

We didn't have premarital counseling. Forty-six years ago, you just got married. Two weeks after our wedding, I said to myself, "I have made a mistake." Nick was a different person once we were married. You know, when you get married and shut the door, you're really who you are. He didn't see any need to hold back, and so we started arguing all the time. I hated conflict; I tried to run from it, but he would chase me down. I would think: "Marriage isn't supposed to be this way." I knew there was something wrong with me: I was so needy. But there was a hardness in Nick—he wasn't very nice. And he couldn't figure me out, because I was always crying. He thought I was the problem; I thought he was a jerk. We had nothing in common; we didn't like to do the same things; he had so much confidence and I had rejection—there was no oneness. It's a miracle we stayed together.

Neither one of us believed in divorce. That's why it scared the fire out of me when we started having so much conflict. I remember thinking, "And I'm supposed to live with this for fifty years?" One time, I was miserable. I wasn't enjoying marriage and thought I was going to have a mental breakdown. Our home was so stressful. Nick wasn't making any money, and we didn't like each other. I didn't know what to do. I had had it, and was at the end of my rope; so I called him at work and said, "I am going to go home to my parents for a few days." Now this is how loving we were then: He said, "No you're not." I said, "Yes I am." And he said, again, "No you're not." So we argued back and forth about that. Then he said, "Okay. But if you do, don't come back." I knew that he said that because he was feeling pressured. His response to pressure was anger, mine was to escape. He was angry that I would even consider leaving. I thought, "Well, I guess I better stay."

When we had a bad argument, I would think the whole marriage was bad. It would be with me for days. But for him, when the argument was over, it was over. I think that if I had left him the devil would have eaten my lunch, convincing me that I had a horrible deal and that I should not go back. Our marriage might have ended, even though we didn't believe in divorce. I think that God used that situation to keep us together. He knew the plans He had for us.

During those first ten years, Nick had amassed serious debt and didn't know how to turn his financial situation around. The tension between him and Callie was constant. In desperation, Callie stood in her living room and cried out to God for help.

God heard her cry and sent Himself to the rescue, by the Holy Spirit.

> *Both of us began to learn about deeper, spiritual things. I started praying every morning, but at the same time, I was trying to change Nick by nagging at him. Then I began asking God to change me. I attended training and learned that when I get into Nick's role, I am out of line. It's sin. I repented. God showed me that I had put myself between Nick and Him. When I got my hands off Nick so that God could work on him, I saw Him change Nick.*

> *We were able to move forward because we were not just going to church, we were getting truth. Our relationship with the Lord changed. We went from a carnal, religious life to a Spirit-filled life. And we had the Baptism of the Holy Spirit, which gave us power to overcome. It brought change and saved our marriage.*

Should we expect to be happy in our marriages? Author Al Janssen, in his book *The Marriage Masterpiece*, says, "Yes, but we don't gain it by demanding it now. We don't obtain it by insisting on self-fulfillment in the relationship. Expectations that my spouse will make me happy inevitably lead to disappointment." This is the tough reality for most of us; recognizing it was the saving grace for Callie and Nick.

> *One of the primary things in marriage is meeting each other's needs. We cannot do that unless we die to ourselves—totally surrender to the Lord and let*

Jesus Christ live in our marriages. I thank God for every terrible situation Nick and I went through. It changed us and it changed our marriage.

As illustrated by Scripture:

They fell down, and there was none to help. Then they cried out to the Lord in their trouble, And He saved them out of their distresses. (Psalm 107: 12–13)

The latter years were conspicuously greater than the former years for Callie and Nick. They were living their marriage by *The Book* instead of by their emotions, and their commitment to oneness in supporting each other paid off. They renewed their minds about what was most important in their relationship, and concluded it was about meeting each other's needs. Willard F. Harley, Jr., concurs: "In marriage, you do things for each other because you care about each other's feelings, not just because you want them done yourself."

When Nick died, unexpectedly, Callie missed him instantly, horribly. Her overwhelming desire was for more—more of the love, the hard-earned oneness she and he had shared, more time with her best friend and ministry partner. Death had come between them too soon. Nights were the hardest. Not just the fearsome darkness but the terrible silence of aloneness, of tears, of "Why now?" thoughts, and the disbelief that someone who was so much a part of her was gone. Yet, beneath her pain was an understanding that there is splendor in God's Word and His creation, which belies any dread that the intended and ultimate destination for love and life is irredeemable death. It is, in fact, a testimony that love and life are a continuum, in Jesus Christ.

Even so, grief is a wrench to a stricken soul. The momentary suffering that befell Callie when Nick died so suddenly was excruciating. There is a fitting quote famously attributed to the ancient Greek playwright Aeschylus. Though his words emerge from a pre-Christian philosophy, they capture the barren feeling of Callie's loss: "Even in our sleep, pain which cannot forget falls drop by drop upon the heart until, in our own despair, against our will, comes wisdom through the awful grace of God."

> *When I look back over the years of our marriage, I am certain that if we had divorced—had not stuck it out and worked it out—we would have missed out on what God had for us as best friends and of oneness. Not only that, had we divorced, we would have devastated our children. Many children of divorce never get over it.*

> *The biggest thing about our marriage problems was that we were able to use them to benefit other marriages through our marriage ministry, because of our testimony of Jesus in our lives.*

"Come and listen, all you who fear God, and I will tell you what God has done for me." (Psalm 66:16) That was the core message of Callie and Nick's ministry. They knew from bitter experience that we can labor on our own and prevent some of the problems typical of marriage, but not all of them. In one fashion or another, problems will keep coming; they have been the bane of marriage since the fall of Eden. However, God's purpose for marriage does not change because we encounter challenges. His desire is that we live together in harmony, in oneness. So, again, the "how" question arises? How do we stay faithful to the vows we take as brides to love and to cherish, in sickness and in health, for better or worse, richer or poorer, till death do us part? How do we overcome the challenges inherent in the vows we make, so that we can experience happiness in our marriages?

"If you and your spouse are in love with each other, you will have a happy marriage. If you are not in love you will feel cheated," says Harley. "So whatever it takes to trigger the feeling of being in love with each other is well worth the effort."

Callie takes it further, to where deep calls to deep:

> *We cannot give up. We have to surrender to the Lord, understanding that it's not about us; it's about God's purpose and that we are nothing without Christ. God instituted marriage for His Kingdom work. If we bail out, we forfeit His fuller plans for our lives.*

Working Out Oneness

How important is it to you to honor your wedding vows and remain in your marriage for life?

_____

Do you view marriage as a cultural or spiritual union? How does your view influence your marriage relationship?

_____

Why do you think God desires oneness in marriage: Matthew 19:5–6?

_____

What has God built into marriage that can only be experienced within the context of a lifelong commitment?

_____

Do you ever feel that you cannot uphold your vow to remain in your marriage? If so, what is your process for persevering, in spite of how you feel? Do you seek counseling, cry out to God, adjust your attitude, or rekindle the flame sputtering away in your bride-memories?

What does Psalm 46:1 mean to you?

In what ways has marriage been an unexpected experience, and yet fulfilled your expectations? How has marriage changed you?

How has marriage deepened your relationship with Jesus?

If you could measure your relationship on a scale of 1 to 10, (10 being strongest) where would it fall? What is your number telling you?

_____

When you examine the expected and unexpected events in your marriage, how does "until death do you part" square with oneness?

_____

When the Vows Break

Jesus replied, "Moses permitted you to divorce your
wives because your hearts were hard. But it was
not this way from the beginning.
(Matthew 19:8 NIV)

What happens when the vows break? The Bible offers insight into a way to view that question: "For whoever keeps the whole law and yet stumbles at just one point is guilty of breaking all of it." (James 2:10) Our wedding vows are as laws established for our marriages, sealed by God and our promise to obey them. Like bricks to a foundation, each one supports the characteristics of bonded love—love that is kind; never envious, boastful, proud, dishonoring, selfish, angry, unforgiving, dishonest, untrustworthy, uncaring, or unreliable. When one is broken, the whole marriage is compromised.

When we divorce, breaking our vows, we become lawbreakers, because our vows are the statutes which work collectively to uphold our marriages. Not only that, when we divorce, we dismiss Matthew 19:6: "Therefore, what God has joined together, let no one separate." Divorce is an act of disobedience. No wonder God hates it. (Malachi 2:16) Yet it seems to me that His hatred of divorce is not just that it is an act of disobedience, but, also, and perhaps primarily, that it is an affront to His standard of oneness. God is one with the Son and Holy Spirit. We are created in His likeness, and in likeness, given into marriage for oneness with our husbands. When we break the bonds of marriage, we contradict God; we disavow His standard of oneness. It is as if we are saying to Him, "Our thoughts and our ways are higher than Yours." Paradoxically, it is because we are prone to operating according to our thoughts and ways that divorce occurs. If our actions and thoughts followed the will of God (and this pertains to our husbands as well), there would be no need for divorce. There would be no adultery, no spousal abuse, no disrespect, no betrayal, no loveless unions, and no abdication of responsibilities within the marriage relationship or the covenant of oneness. These are the insidious behaviors that destroy oneness and make divorce necessary. If these treacheries to marriage did not exist, all of us would be happily married and able to make it to the finish line.

Every divorced couple has a different story to tell. But the fact remains that divorce is the chief enemy of God's plan for marriage. God is a family Man, inextricably united with the Holy Spirit and Jesus Christ. His design for marriage is intended to reflect His divine image of family. Husbands and wives are supposed to be unified in an insoluble, inviolate, unbreakable bond, with the primary purpose of producing children. The Bible states in Malachi 2:15, "But did He not make them one, having a remnant of the Spirit? And why one? He seeks godly offspring. Therefore, take heed to your spirit, and let none deal treacherously with the wife of his youth." Nevertheless, and notwithstanding the inerrancy of Scripture, marriage is a hard and rutted passage from self to selfless. It is like the Preamble to the Constitution: always striving to form a more perfect union. Divorce is not and was never supposed to be an option, except for sexual immorality. (Matthew 5:31–32) Therein lies the problem, because when we are hurting in our marriages, our survival instincts tend more toward extrication than submission. This inclination is greatly advantaged by the *no-fault* provisions for expediting divorce, making it easy for us to bail out due to *irreconcilable differences*. But untying the knot has not always been the quick and easy-fresh start, clean slate experience that it is today. I can remember the time when the word *divorce* was unspeakable. People whispered it as if it were a dreaded disease to be shrouded in hushed tones. It was one of many words that were considered to be indelicate. For example, a woman was not pregnant, she was *expecting*, or she was *in a family way*; she did not have her period, she had her *monthly*, and so on. In those days, taboos modified language and behavior with a distinct dividing line between adults and children, the latter never to be included in grown-up matters. I remember the moment a neighbor crossed that line and told me that my favorite aunt and uncle were divorcing. It struck me so hard that I still hold the picture of that moment clearly in my mind. I was young then about eight years old. It was a warm, bright day in early summer. The sun sat high in the afternoon sky, putting on a brazen display of its power over the mill haze that always hung in the Pittsburgh air, before the city was transformed from an industrial town built from steel production to a world-class medical and technology center. I was sitting on the concrete step in front of the door to the apartment building where our family lived at the time, waiting for a playmate to join me in a game of jacks or to hunt unsuspecting bumble bees settling on the honeysuckle blossoms, so that we could trap them in our empty jelly jars. A woman approaching the building stopped where I was sitting, leaned toward me, and in a cloaked voice said something to the effect of, "I hear your aunt and uncle are divorcing." I raced up the three flights of stairs to my apartment and asked my mother if what the woman said was true. In my young mind, it couldn't be true. No one in my family was divorced. I don't recall my mother actually answering my question. What I recall vividly is her expressed outrage that that woman would speak that word to me, would tell me a thing like that—something that should have stuck to the roof of her mouth, something that was adult and private. I do recall my mother telling me not to repeat what the woman said to me. Her admonishment was clear, spoken in rueful tones that came with a piercing look every child recognizes as a message of certain consequences for disobedience. I can only guess that any conversation about the breakup was confined to pillow talk between my parents, because there was never an open discussion, not in my presence. I have no memory of when the divorce became a fact instead of a question. It happened quietly. It was as if all the adults had gathered secretly to bury the subject behind the building on some moonless night while the children slept. To be divorced in those days was tantamount to moral failure—something so repugnant and irreverent that churches expelled couples who dared to dissolve their marriages. Top-level positions in companies, corporations, and public service agencies often were denied to divorcees; and many of the newly single were politely removed from the social calendars of their friends.

That early experience of near silence about divorce solidified in me the seriousness of it. So when I was standing at the altar repeating my vows, I had that forever in my mind. That got tested very quickly. I wish I could say that, except for the incident when I told my mother I had made a mistake in getting married, I never again contemplated a way out. But I cannot. There was a time when "out" was exactly what I wanted, not because I didn't love Morris but because I was tired of feeling like an ellipsis in my relationship with him. I thought living separately with peace of mind was better than dangling from what had become for me a life of incongruities. What stopped me were the vows—not so much what I had pledged to him (anger and frustration can obscure just about anything, including marriage vows), but rather my covenant with God to honor my marriage and remain in it for better or worse, richer or poorer, in sickness and in health, and to love and cherish my husband till death do us part. What's more, I had children who at one point were alarmingly aware of and vocal about our crumbling state. I didn't want them to endure a broken family nor did I want to leave a legacy of divorce for them. So I stayed and prayed and toughed it out. I chose to uphold my vows, brittle as they were, and trust Jesus to heal our marriage and my heart. I say *my heart* because I knew that I needed to be free from anger, and I knew that it would take patience (of which I had little). I had to "let go and let God" as they say—let Him go to work in me. I am glad that I did. I am glad that I am still with Morris—the one I love and have loved my whole life.

But for a time, it was hard for me to allow Jesus access to the deep places where I had stockpiled rage. A part of me wanted to preserve it for some kind of tortured satisfaction. I will admit that I can hold on to anger for a long time, once I reach boiling point. But the bigger part of me did not want to do that, not just because of the bitterness that would result but "because human anger does not produce the righteousness that God desires." (James 1:20) I needed to get it together for my sake and leave Morris to Jesus. The irony is that when we were planning our wedding, we were perceived as being an ideal couple. I remember Father Parker (who married us) telling Morris and me during our premarital counseling that if we could not make it no one could. He was that confident because he had known us since we were children in the church, and he knew the closeness of our families. We had a lot in common, more than most couples starting out. Yet we came right to the edge of not making it. Father Parker would have been surprised to see how divided we had become; I was surprised. I am grateful that God is faithful and that nothing is too difficult for Him. (Genesis 18:14 and Jeremiah 32:27) He healed my heart—not instantly, but over time, as I understood that hardness had taken the place of anger. I surrendered my emotions to Him and determined that I would live my marriage by *The Book*.

"There is a growing sense among some that marriage is a nice thing to have if it fits your lifestyle. If not, there are alternatives," writes Al Janessen in *The Marriage Masterpiece*. Perhaps it is because in today's society almost everything is temporary and everyone wants to escape pain, even (and especially) the pain of marriage. The most prescribed medicine for that pain is divorce. But that remedy flies in the face of God's plan for marriage. For it is He Who "created man in His own image; in the image of God He created him; male and female He created them. Then God blessed them and God said to them, 'Be fruitful and multiply; fill the earth and subdue it...'" (Genesis 1:27–28) From the beginning, God had marriage in mind—a covenantal union between husbands and wives in which oneness can be seen just as clearly as He exhibits oneness with the Holy Spirit and Jesus Christ. He would never divorce Himself from His family. In our human weakness, we do it all the time. We suffer the stain and cost of it and continue in an effort to make the best of it. Studies show that divorce, particularly when children are involved, inflicts long-lasting emotional and psychological damage on the family. In an article published by the *Center for Arizona Policy*, the perils of divorce are articulated in sobering detail. "Over 20 years of sociological research on married couples, divorcees, and their children has shown without a doubt that divorce has an overwhelmingly negative impact not only on the divorcing couple, but also on children of divorce, who bear scars into their adult lives. Rather than being a way to escape unhappy marriages, divorce has become a way to enforce lifelong unhappiness." Is it any wonder that God hates divorce and has spoken about it unequivocally throughout the Bible, in both Old and New Testaments?

Yet, sometimes, divorce is not only desirable, it is necessary for our stability, safety, and the protection of our children. Although it is true that God hates divorce, it is also true that He is a forgiving God Who does not hate us because of divorce. Divorce is a heartache for God and us. It is not an unforgivable sin. There is only one unforgivable act that Scripture identifies as sin, and divorce is not it. (Mark 3:28–29) God's standard for marriage is love through oneness that is both loving and honoring. It is not His will for wives and children to be held hostage to the miseries of abuse and abjection, whether physical, emotional, or psychological. He has laid out His expectations of husbands clearly in 1Peter 3:7: "In the same way, you husbands, live with your wives in an understanding way (with great gentleness and tact, and with an intelligent regard for the marriage relationship), as with someone physically weaker, since she is a woman. Show her honor and respect as a fellow heir of the grace of life, so that your prayers will not be hindered or ineffective." (AMP)

We can hope for change and seek Jesus for divine intervention, knowing that "with God nothing will be impossible" (Luke 1:37), however, not every spouse is willing to change. Saul didn't become Paul until he was knocked off his high horse and struck blind; and the young rich man would not let go of his money, even for Jesus.

Leslie knows a thing or two about waiting in vain for change. She waited for years for any inkling that Josh was changing, praying all the while, seeking help through Christian counseling (he refused to go), and doing everything she could to be an excellent wife. She firmly believed that God could transform anyone. Surely, the fact that her husband was a liar and an adulterer did not mean that he was beyond the reach of Jesus. But like the young rich man who would not give up his money, Josh was not willing to be transformed. The duplicitous person he was when he and Leslie were planning their marriage is the person he remained throughout their marriage.

> *Before we were married, he impregnated someone else. He told me that himself! I was so angry. I just started throwing things at him. He was very remorseful. But I felt hurt and conflicted. I talked with my father about it and he said, "Honey, I can't tell you what to do, but if you choose to leave him, don't go back to him. If you choose to stay with him, don't bring it up again." I couldn't imagine my life without him. I loved him. He showed me that he loved me and wanted me to be his wife.*

So Leslie forgave him and put her mind on their future together. There were many adjustments she would need to make as his wife. Josh had signed with a major league baseball team, which meant he would be away from home for weeks and months at a time during game season. Baseball was Josh's passion and had been from the moment she met him, when they were students at the University of Alabama. What she did not expect was that his career would become a cover for his hidden life with other women.

His habitual indiscretions were crushing to her. They piled up like a stack of Jenga blocks in the middle of their marriage and strained toward the moment when that one block too many would bring the whole thing down.

Still, there were children to consider, most especially their young daughter who was profoundly, developmentally impaired, requiring round-the-clock care. Leslie needed Josh, but more than that, she believed that there was still a chance that he could be the husband described in Proverbs 5:18–19, which says: "Let your fountain be blessed, and rejoice with the wife of your youth. As a loving deer and a graceful doe, let her breasts satisfy you at all times; and always be enraptured with her love."

I have come to realize that I got married; Josh did not. I don't know if he didn't have a desire to be right or didn't know how! When I married him, I married for good. I didn't want what happened to my parents to happen to me. They divorced when I was in the tenth grade. There was so much chaos and turmoil in our household during that time. But even though my parents divorced, I had a strict, Christian upbringing. Growing up, I went to a Catholic school and attended a Baptist church. I went to church every Sunday and was faithful in reading my Bible and praying. Church was a big thing. If my dad allowed me to sleep in, it was because I had a tough week and needed the rest. If I wasn't dying, I went to church. When Josh and I began dating, we would read the Bible together. After a few months, he asked to go to church with me. I thought, "Lord, You brought someone who wants to grow with me in my Christian walk!" I was nine-teen—so naïve.

It took twelve years of heartache and tears before that final block was pulled from the stack, bringing down their marriage and scattering the pieces too far to be recovered. Josh's vain pursuits had pushed carpe diem to its most callous edge. Divorce seemed to be the only, reasonable option.

> *I sensed that something was wrong. Call it intu-ition, the Holy Spirit, I could feel it; but I didn't have proof. I could feel it in our communication, his responses, even in the bedroom—things were changing. I started praying, asking God to reveal what was wrong and what I needed to do to correct it. I kept hoping and praying that he would turn his life around—that's what kept me in the marriage over the years: hoping and praying. I would think about what I would do if I left him? By then we had two children. I had no work experience, and I had not finished my degree. All these factors were in my head, working against me. I would think, "If I leave, I will have nothing!" One time I happened to be in a conversation with someone who didn't know that I was married to Josh. The conversation moved to professional sports and the guys who were involved with other women. Josh's name came up in connec-tion with a child—not a child of ours, a child he had with someone else. Imagine it! Someone I did not know was talking like that about my life? I hired a private investigator to find out if what she said was true. It was. Not only that, he was cheating in other*

ways with other women. I had been faithful to him all those years, had forgiven him again and again. I did not deserve to be treated like that. I loved him, but I was fed up. I filed for divorce.

I never wanted to be divorced. I made a vow to myself that I would never divorce, no matter what. I would work through it and do whatever it takes. But guess what? It takes two. I was focused on the stigma of divorce and that God doesn't like divorce. But we were unequally yoked. Josh has no problem going through life hurting people and being disconnected from it.

I am in a much better place now. I rely on my faith for everything. I relied on God's hand of grace to cover me so that I could push through and detox from all the dysfunction. I learned through therapy that I had held Josh to the same standard I saw in my father. He was an amazing father! I thought every man was like that. Once I let go of that expectation, I felt free.

Holding on to an unloving spouse in a demoralizing marriage does not honor us as wives nor does it honor God or His purpose for marriage. God is merciful and has grace for those of us who have experienced divorce. We have to remember that Jesus carried all our transgressions with Him to the cross, including our broken vows. "Therefore there is now no condemnation for those who are in Christ Jesus." (Romans 8:1) But divorce has consequences. Even when it is necessary, divorce is out of God's order. God designed marriage to be an expression of love—love like His: kind, patient, encouraging, humble, considerate, selfless, and self-controlled. But when marriage becomes a stronghold for cruelty, contempt, disrespect, deception, rigidity, selfishness, unfaithfulness, violence, and other abuses which devalue or ignore our worth as women, wives, and mothers, then the marriage relationship, also, is out of God's order. In that failed state, when offending husbands refuse to repent and put an end to their destructive behaviors, making it impossible for healing to occur and honor to be restored, God's grace is sufficient to cover divorce "for all have sinned and fall short of the glory of God, and all are justified freely by His grace through the redemption that came by Christ Jesus." (Romans 3:23–24)

Working Out Oneness

When you married, did you have forever in mind? Do you still have forever in mind?

_____

Have you ever wanted out of your marriage? If so, what caused you to stay?

_____

What do you regard as the most egregious offense to your marriage?

_____

Do you think that the easy divorce laws encourage couples to take marriage less seriously than they should? If so, how?

_____

Have you or anyone in your family experienced divorce? If so, how has it affected your life?

_____

Why do you think our culture has been so successful at changing Judeo-Christian teachings?

_____

Why do you think God uses such strong language in Malachi 2:16 to convey His feelings about divorce?

_____

If you are now or have ever been divorced, how has it affected your thinking about marriage, about husbands, and about being a wife?

_____

Do you have regrets? If so, what would you do differently?

_____

In what ways have you grown because of divorce?

_____

If you have children, what has been the impact of your divorce on them?

Why do you think God views adultery as the most egregious offense to marriage and the one for which He allows divorce?

Do you believe that God forgives us when we divorce? Do you feel His forgiveness? In what ways do you feel forgiven?

Forgiveness

Nothing cries out for forgiveness more than the pain of divorce. Forgiveness can be tough to embrace because it means we have to humble ourselves and let go of our desire for retribution. But forgiveness is central to moving on in God with an unburdened heart. A broken marriage hurts because it is an amputation of our covenant with God and our husbands. Just as the stump of a severed leg gives witness to loss, and the nerve endings that were once connected to a whole limb continue to react to what is no longer there, a broken marriage leaves evidence in our hearts of the lost oneness. Inevitably, there is regret. There is regret because of the part we played in destroying our marriages, for the men we chose to marry, for the pain they inflicted on us, for having a wrong motive for marrying, or a misconception of what a covenantal marriage requires; or, for the plain and simple fact that our marriages failed. We need to forgive ourselves and our ex-husbands as well. Otherwise, the hurt lingers in our souls, dragging the past with us like a phantom limb throbbing with memories of our pain, hindering our efforts to move forward toward a healthy heart and mind.

Forgiveness does not mean that we no longer remember the pain we felt going through a divorce. But remembering that we once experienced pain is not the same as living with unresolved pain. Pain is our signal that healing is needed. Healing requires that we recognize the source of pain so that it can receive the proper attention. In fact, attending to our pain means we must remember how and why it began, because the remedy is freedom. We gain freedom when we learn from our experiences; we become wiser, and wisdom is godly empowerment. We become stronger because we don't have the pain of the past sapping our energy for the future, making us susceptible to seeking ill-thought relationships to soothe our wounded hearts. We become lighter because we are in God's will and doing the work of Colossians 3:13, forgiving one another and enjoying the freedom the Lord offers, when we obey Him.

However, freedom through forgiveness is a process. How long it takes is individual. But it begins when we face ourselves, not as an exercise of self-pity, rather of self-awareness, and a willingness to forgive ourselves. We cannot float on the surface waves of forgiveness. We have to take a deep breath and dive to the bottom so that it can engulf us, silence us, until we feel the airless flood of God's peace washing over us, freeing us. It's uncomfortable, but worthwhile. Adrienne can attest to that. Before her marriage to Jeffrey, she had taken the courageous step of confronting herself about her past. She was very familiar with divorce and the aftereffects. So she embarked on a personal journey into the deep places of her mind where attitudes about marriage and commitment were tucked away, yet close enough to seep into her consciousness. She did not like what she saw. What she realized was that, in her mind, marriage was not a union of oneness. It was a provisional commitment—a personalized version of the world's idea of marriage rather than God's plan. In short, what she saw was a secular view of marriage, which translated to: *disposable*. That self-encounter changed her thinking and drew her closer to God and into alignment with His perspective as laid out in Romans 12:2: "Do not conform to the pattern of this world, but be transformed by the renewing of your mind. Then you will be able to test and approve what God's will is—His good, pleasing and perfect will." (NIV)

> *"I used to think that I would remain married as long as it was working. When it stopped working, it was over. I moved on," she said. "I got married with that kind of mindset—it was the `throw-away' mentality of that time. I didn't understand the deep things of the Christian faith. My faith was superficial. Once I understood what God says about divorce, well...* (she stopped, her unfinished thought clearly articulated in her raised brow). *I had to change. I am not the same person I was back then. Sometimes I see friends who have been married for forty years, with memories of making it through good times and hard times. They have children and grandchildren and I feel a mixture of envy and admiration. I will never have that because of the choices I made. I regret that. I made a decision that if I ever married again, it would be a commitment for life. I would not divorce. There is truth and there is reality. The truth is that God's plan is for marriage to be a lifelong commitment. Reality is what we experience as we put God's plan into practice.*

The Bible says in John 10:10, "The thief comes only to steal and kill and destroy; I have come that they may have life, and have it to the full." (NIV) Adrienne cannot get back what divorce stole from her. But what she has in Jesus Christ is forgiveness. God has honored her willingness to turn from her old ways of thinking and live by *The Book*. He has given her a renewed and full life in a covenantal marriage to Jeffrey, with Jesus Christ at the center.

Like Adrienne, Leslie says she wishes she had done some things differently, particularly with respect to her relationship with Josh: times when she might have been more circumspect but, instead, dropped her guard and allowed her emotions to rule. But that's behind her. God healed her heart and renewed her hope for the future.

Every one of us has regrets whether we are married or divorced. What matters is what we do with them. Do we wander around in a wilderness of self-reproach, feeling like victims, dragging around a heavy heart filled with bitterness or shame? No! We accept that we made mistakes, that we caused hurt, and that we have been hurt. We release ourselves and our husbands (present or ex) from the unloving acts, the wounding words, the disappointments, the neglect, the indiscretions, the betrayals, the dishonor, and all the rest of it. Moreover, we refuse to indulge the specters of our outrage, but rather welcome the liberating love of Jesus Christ Who is able to carry our burdens. In other words, we emerge salted, not salty. As David A. Seamands said in *Healing of Memories*, "We cannot long ingest and integrate hidden resentments, anymore than our stomachs can digest and incorporate bits of broken glass." He further describes in his workbook *Healing for Damaged Emotions* what he calls the "Fearsome Foursome of Unforgiveness." These are guilt, resentment, striving, and anxiety, which produce stress, conflict, and emotional problems. He goes on to say, "Forgiveness is NOT excusing or minimizing the wrong that has been done. Rather, it is consciously acknowledging the wrong and purposely choosing to pardon the person by whom you've been wronged." I would expand that by inverting his statement to include our need for God's forgiveness, not just for the hurt we know we caused, but also the unrecognized hurt. We need the Light of Christ on the hidden things so that we do not give Satan an opportunity to sneak up on us with the Fearsome Foursome and steal the peace we have achieved following the stress of divorce, or destroy the loving feelings we have reignited after a season of conflict with our husbands.

But is it really possible to forgive like this? Can we wipe the slate clean without leaving the tiniest bit of residue from the past on ourselves? Yes, we can. We open our Bible and meditate on God's truth, praying earnestly and surrendering our hearts to God Who is holy and just to cleanse us of all unforgiveness toward the men who were or are our husbands. When Jesus said to his disciples in Matthew 6:9–13, "This is how you should pray," He was emphatic in His instruction about how to go to God in prayer. He laid out seven key elements for prayer line-by-line. In verse 12, He said, "And forgive us our debts as we forgive our debtors." Jesus was speaking to us also. We are His twenty-first century disciples, and we need to pray for a for-giving heart, daily, because forgiveness comes both from the divine will of God and a willful action on our part. We have to choose to forgive by taking every thought and emotion captive to the obedience of God, and putting our trust in His character, not in ours. That is how we do it—we shake off our anger—our outrage—and press into our Savior. It is not easy. But God re-quires it, and we have no excuse. Like the disciples of old, we are being refined daily to reflect His image. God has made us heirs to His promise that He will complete the good work He began in us until the day of Jesus Christ. (Philippians 1:6) We are accountable to Him alone for our attitudes and behaviors, not those of our husbands'. Therefore, we have no reason to suffer regrets; no reason to harbor unforgiveness. They belong at the foot of the Cross, covered by the blood of Jesus.

Working Out Oneness

What are you doing to move forward in God's plan for your life?

_____

In what areas of your marriage are you stuck in unforgiveness?

_____

How sincerely do you seek Jesus for wisdom regarding your character flaws and how they contribute to marriage conflict?

_____

Do you hold on to unforgiveness because of disappointment or anger?

_____

How does Colossians 3:13 factor into your thinking about forgiveness?

_____

What attitudes or behaviors do you express that are your signals to forgive or that you need forgiveness?

Where are you in your process toward freedom from the pain of unforgiveness?

How close are you to peace and contentment?

How committed are you to aligning your emotions with the heart of God, manifesting the truth of His Word by living your life for Him, by The Book?

Living Marriage by the Book

For whatever was written in earlier times was
written for our instruction, so that through
perseverance and the encouragement of the
Scriptures we might have hope.
(Romans 15:4)

Courtship and Dating

Psalm 37:4

Delight yourself also in the Lord, and He shall give you the desires of your heart.

Proverbs 4:23

Above all else, guard your heart, for everything you do flows from it. (NIV)

Proverbs 11:22

Like a gold ring in a pig's snout is a beautiful woman who shows no discretion. (NIV)

Proverbs 12:26

The righteous choose their friends carefully, but the way of the wicked leads them astray. (NIV)

Proverbs 22:24

Make no friendship with an angry man, and with a furious man do not go.

Proverbs 31:10

Who can find a virtuous wife? For her worth *is* far above rubies.

Proverbs 31:30

Charm *is* deceitful and beauty *is* passing, but a woman *who* fears the Lord, she shall be praised.

Song of Solomon 2:7

I charge you, O daughters of Jerusalem, by the gazelles or by the does of the field, do not stir up nor awaken love until it pleases.

1 Corinthians 10:13

No temptation has overtaken you except such as is common to man; but God is faithful, Who will not allow you to be tempted beyond what you are able, but with the temptation will also make a way of escape, that you may be able to bear it.

1 Corinthians 15:33

Do not be misled: Bad company corrupts good character. (NIV)

1 Corinthians 6:18

Flee sexual immorality. Every sin that a man does is outside the body, but he who commits sexual immorality sins against his own body.

2 Corinthians 11:2

For I am jealous for you with godly jealousy. For I have betrothed you to one husband, that I may present *you as* a chaste virgin to Christ.

2 Corinthians 6:14

Do not be unequally yoked together with unbelievers. For what fellowship has righteousness with lawlessness? And what communion has light with darkness?

Romans 13:12

The night is almost gone, and the day is near. Therefore let us lay aside the deeds of darkness and put on the armor of light. (NASB)

Galatians 5:16

I say then: Walk in the Spirit, and you shall not fulfill the lust of the flesh.

1 Thessalonians 4:3–6

It is God's will that you should be sanctified: that you should avoid sexual immorality; that each of you should learn to control your own body in a way that is holy and honorable, not in passionate lust like the pagans, who do not know God; and that in this matter no one should wrong or take advantage of a brother or sister. The Lord will punish all those who commit such sins, as we told you and warned you before. (NIV)

2 Timothy 2:22

Flee also youthful lusts; but pursue righteousness, faith, love, peace with those who call on the Lord out of a pure heart.

1 Peter 1:15–16

 But just as he who called you is holy, so be holy in all you do; for it is written: "Be holy, because I am holy." (NIV)

1 John 2:16

For all that *is* in the world—the lust of the flesh, the lust of the eyes, and the pride of life—is not of the Father but is of the world.

Amos 3:3

Can two walk together, unless they are agreed?

Marry Me

Genesis 2:18

And the Lord God said, "It is not good that man should be alone; I will make him a helper comparable to him."

Genesis 34:12

Make the price for the bride and the gift I am to bring as great as you like, and I'll pay whatever you ask me. Only give me the young woman as my wife." (NIV)

Psalm 34:3

Oh, magnify the Lord with me, and let us exalt His name together.

Proverbs 5:28

Let your wife be a fountain of blessing for you. Rejoice in the wife of your youth. (NTL)

Proverbs 12:4

An excellent wife is the—crown of her husband, but she who causes shame is like rottenness in his bones.

Proverbs 19:14

Houses and riches are an inheritance from fathers, but a prudent wife is from the Lord.

Proverbs 18:22

He who finds a wife finds what is good and receives favor from the Lord.

Proverbs 31:10–12

A wife of noble character who can find? She is worth far more than rubies. Her husband has full confidence in her and lacks nothing of value. She brings him good, not harm, all the days of her life. (NIV)

Ecclesiastes 4:9–12

Two are better than one because they have a good return for their labor. For if either of them falls, the one will lift up his companion. But woe to the one who falls when there is not another to lift him up. Furthermore, if two lie down together they keep warm, but how can one be warm alone? And if one can overpower him who is alone, two can resist him. A cord of three strands is not quickly torn apart.(NASB)

Song of Solomon 2:10

My beloved spoke, and said to me: "Rise up, my love, my fair one, and come away...."

Song of Solomon 4:7

You are all fair, my love, and there is no spot in you.

Song of Solomon 4:9

You have stolen my heart, my sister, my bride; you have stolen my heart with one glance of your eyes, with one jewel of you necklace.

Song of Solomon 6:10

Who is this that appears like the dawn, fair as the moon, bright as the sun, majestic as the stars in procession? (NIV)

Song of Solomon 8:6–7

Set me as a seal upon your heart, as a seal upon your arm; for love is as strong as death, jealousy as cruel as the grave; its flames are flames of fire, a most vehement flame. Many waters cannot quench love, nor can the floods drown it. If a man would give for love all the wealth of his house, it would be utterly despised.

Jeremiah 33:11

Give thanks to the Lord Almighty, for the Lord is good; His love endures forever. (NIV)

Hosea 2:19–20

I will betroth you to Me forever; yes, I will betroth you to Me in righteousness and justice, in loving kindness and mercy; I will betroth you to Me in faithfulness, and you shall know the Lord .

Amos 3:3

Can two walk together, unless they are agreed?

Malachi 2:15

But did He not make them one, having a remnant of the Spirit? And why one? He seeks godly offspring. Therefore take heed to your spirit, and let none deal treacherously with the wife of your youth.

Galatians 3:15

Brothers and sisters, let me take an example from everyday life. Just as no one can set aside or add to a human covenant that has been duly established, so it is in this case. (NIV)

Here Comes the Bride

Genesis 2:24

For this reason a man shall leave his father and his mother, and be joined to his wife; and they shall become one flesh. (NASB)

Isaiah 62:5

As a young man marries a young woman, so will your Builder marry you; as a bridegroom rejoices over his bride, so will your God rejoice over you. (NIV)

Ezekiel 16:8

And when I passed by again, I saw that you were old enough for love. So I wrapped my cloak around you to cover your nakedness and declared my marriage vows. I made a covenant with you, says the Sovereign Lord, and you became mine. (NLT)

Proverbs 3:3–4

Let not mercy and truth forsake you; bind them around your neck, write them on the tablet of your heart, and so find favor and high esteem in the sight of God and man.

Proverbs 19:14

Houses and riches *are* an inheritance from fathers, but a prudent wife *is* from the Lord.

Proverbs 30:18–19

There are three things which are too wonderful for me, yes, four which I do not understand: the way of an eagle in the air, the way of a serpent on a rock, the way of a ship in the midst of the sea, and the way of a man with a virgin.

Proverbs 31:10–11

An excellent wife, who can find? For her worth is far above jewels. The heart of her husband trusts in her, and he will have no lack of gain. (NASB)

Song of Solomon 4:11

Your lips, my bride, drip honey; Honey and milk are under your tongue, and the fragrance of you garments is like the fragrance of Lebanon. (NASB)

Song of Solomon 4:16

Awake, north wind, and come, south wind! Blow on my garden, that its fragrance may spread everywhere. Let my beloved come into his garden and taste its choice fruits. (NIV)

Song of Solomon 6:3

I am my beloved's, and my beloved is mine. He feeds his flock among the lilies.

Song of Solomon 7:10

I am my beloved's, and his desire is toward me.

Song of Solomon 2:18

The voice of my beloved! Behold, he comes, leaping upon the mountains, skipping upon the hills.

Mark 10:6–9

But from the beginning of the creation, God "made them male and female. For this reason a man shall leave his father and mother and be joined to his wife, and the two shall become one flesh"; so then they are no longer two, but one flesh. Therefore what God has joined together, let not man separate.

John 3:27

John answered and said, "A man can receive nothing unless it has been given to him from heaven.

John 13:34–35

A new commandment I give to you, that you love one another; as I have loved you, that you also love one another. By this all will know that you are My disciples, if you have love for one another.

Romans 15:5–6

Now may the God of patience and comfort grant you to be like-minded toward one another, according to Christ Jesus, that you may with one mind and one mouth glorify the God and Father of our Lord Jesus Christ.

1 Corinthians 7:2

But because there is so much sexual immorality, each man should have his own wife, and each woman should have her own husband. (NLT)

Ephesians 5:2

And walk in the way of love, just as Christ loved us and gave himself up for us as a fragrant offering and sacrifice to God. (NIV)

Ephesian 5:21-24

Submit to one another out of reverence for Christ. Wives, submit to your husbands as to the Lord. For the husband is the head of the wife as Christ is the head of the church, his body, of which he is the Savior. Now as the church submits to Christ, so also wives should submit to their husbands in everything. (NIV)

Ephesians 5:25

Husbands, love your wives, just as Christ also loved the church and gave Himself for her.

Hebrews 13:4

Marriage is honorable among all, and the bed undefiled; but fornicators and adulterers God will judge.

1 Peter 3:1–4

Wives, likewise, be submissive to your own husbands, that even if some do not obey the word, they, without a word, may be won by the conduct of their wives, when they observe your chaste conduct accompanied by fear. Do not let your adornment be merely outward—arranging the hair, wearing gold, or putting on fine apparel—rather let it be the hidden person of the heart, with the incorruptible beauty of a gentle and quiet spirit, which is very precious in the sight of God.

To Love and to Cherish

Ruth 1:16–17

Entreat me not to leave you, or to turn back from following after you; for wherever you go, I will go; and wherever you lodge, I will lodge; your people shall be my people, and your God, my God. Where you die, I will die, and there will I be buried. The Lord do so to me, and more also, if anything but death parts you and me.

Psalm 85:10

Love and faithfulness meet together; righteousness and peace kiss each other. (NIV)

Proverbs 15:17

Better is a dinner of herbs where love is, than a fatted calf with hatred.

Proverbs 20:6–7

Most men will proclaim each his own goodness, but who can find a faithful man? The righteous man walks in his integrity; his children are blessed after him.

Song of Solomon 5:16

His mouth is sweetness itself; he is desirable in every way. Such, O women of Jerusalem, is my lover, my friend. (NLT)

Romans 12:10

Be devoted to one another in brotherly love; give preference to one another in honor. (NASB)

1 Corinthians 7:3

Let the husband render to his wife the affection due her, and likewise also the wife to her husband.

1 Corinthians 10:24

Let no one seek his own, but each one the other's well-being.

1 Corinthians 16:14

Do everything in love. (NIV)

Ephesians 5:1–2

Therefore be imitators of God, as beloved children; and walk in love, just as Christ also loved you and gave Himself up for us, an offering and a sacrifice to God as a fragrant aroma. (NASB)

Ephesians 5:22–24

Wives, submit to your own husbands, as to the Lord. For the husband is head of the wife, as also Christ is head of the church; and He is the Savior of the body. Therefore, just as the church is subject to Christ, so let the wives be to their own husbands in everything.

Philippians 1:9–10

And this I pray, that your love may abound still more and more in real knowledge and all discernment, so that you may approve the things that are excellent, in order to be sincere and blameless until the day of Christ. (NASB)

Thessalonians 3:12–13

And may the Lord make you increase and abound in love to one another and to all, just as we do to you, so that He may establish your hearts blameless in holiness before our God and Father at the coming of our Lord Jesus Christ with all His saints.

2 Thessalonians 3:5

May the Lord direct your hearts into God's love and Christ's perseverance. (NIV)

1 John 3:18

My little children, let us not love in word or in tongue, but in deed and in truth.

1 John 4:16

We have come to know and have believed the love which God has for us. God is love, and the one who abides in love abides in God, and God abides in him. (NASB)

1 John 4:18

There is no fear in love; but perfect love casts out fear, because fear involves torment. But he who fears has not been made perfect in love.

1 Peter 5:14

Greet one another with a kiss of love.

For Better or Worse

Job 23:10

But He knows the way that I take; when He has tested me, I shall come forth as gold.

Psalm 32:7

You are my hiding place; you shall preserve me from trouble; you shall surround me with songs of deliverance.

Psalm 57:1

Be merciful to me, O God, be merciful to me! For my soul trusts in You; and in the shadow of Your wings I will make my refuge, until these calamities have passed by.

Psalm 66:10

For You, O God, have tested us; you have refined us as silver is refined.

Proverbs 12:4

An excellent wife *is* the crown of her husband, but she who causes shame *is* like rottenness in his bones.

Proverbs 14:29

Whoever is patient has great understanding, but one who is quick-tempered displays folly. (NIV)

Proverbs 17:3

The refining pot *is* for silver and the furnace for gold, but the Lord tests the hearts.

Proverbs 19:13

A foolish son *is* the ruin of his father, and the contentions of a wife *are* a continual dripping.

Proverbs 21:19

Better to dwell in the wilderness, than with a contentious and angry woman.

Proverbs 22:1

A good name is to be chosen rather than great riches, loving favor rather than silver and gold.

Proverbs 25:24

It is better to dwell in a corner of a housetop, than in a house shared with a contentious woman.

Proverbs 27:15

A continual dripping on a very rainy day and a contentious woman are alike.

Proverbs 29:11

A fool always loses his temper, but a wise man holds it back. (NASB)

Matthew 6:14–15

For if you forgive other people when they sin against you, your heavenly Father will also forgive you. But if you do not forgive others their sins, your Father will not forgive your sins. (NIV)

Matthew 11:28–30

Come to Me, all you who labor and are heavy laden, and I will give you rest. Take My yoke upon you and learn from Me, for I am gentle and lowly in heart, and you will find rest for your souls. For My yoke is easy and My burden is light.

John 16:33

These things I have spoken to you, that in Me you may have peace. In the world you will have tribulation; but be of good cheer, I have overcome the world.

Acts 3:19–20

Repent, then, and turn to God, so that your sins may be wiped out, that times of refreshing may come from the Lord, and that He may send the Messiah, who has been appointed for you— even Jesus. (NIV)

Romans 12:9–10

Don't just pretend to love others. Really love them. Hate what is wrong. Hold tightly to what is good. Love each other with genuine affection, and take delight in honoring each other. (NLT)

1 Corinthians 13:2

If I have the gift of prophecy, and know all mysteries and all knowledge; and if I have all faith, so as to remove mountains, but do not have love, I am nothing. (NASB)

1 Corinthians 13:4–7

Love suffers long and is kind; love does not envy; love does not parade itself, is not puffed up; does not behave rudely, does not seek its own, is not provoked, thinks no evil; does not rejoice in iniquity, but rejoices in the truth; bears all things, believes all things, hopes all things, endures all things.

1 Corinthians 13:13

And now abide faith, hope, love, these three; but the greatest of these *is* love.

2 Corinthians 10:5

We break down every thought and proud thing that puts itself up against the wisdom of God. We take hold of every thought and make it obey Christ. (NIV)

2 Corinthians 5:17–19

Therefore, if anyone is in Christ, he is a new creation; old things have passed away; behold, all things have become new. Now all things are of God, who has reconciled us to Himself through Jesus Christ, and has given us the ministry of reconciliation, that is, that God was in Christ reconciling the world to Himself, not imputing their trespasses to them, and has committed to us the word of reconciliation.

Ephesians 4:2–3

Always be humble and gentle. Be patient with each other, making allowance for each other's faults because of your love. Make every effort to keep yourselves united in the Spirit, binding yourselves together with peace. (NLT)

Ephesians 4:31–32

Let all bitterness, wrath, anger, clamor, and evil speaking be put away from you, with all malice. And be kind to one another, tenderhearted, forgiving one another, even as God in Christ forgave you.

Ephesians 5:21

Submit to one another out of reverence for Christ. (NIV)

Ephesians 5:33

Nevertheless let each one of you in particular so love his own wife as himself, and let the wife see that she respects her husband.

Ephesians 6:13

Therefore, take up the full armor of God, so that you will be able to resist in the evil day, and having done everything, to stand firm. (NASB)

Hebrews 4:15

For we do not have a High Priest who cannot sympathize with our weaknesses, but was in all points tempted as we are, yet without sin.

Ephesians 4:26

And "don't sin by letting anger control you." Don't let the sun go down while you are still angry. (NLT)

Philippians 4:13

I can do all things through Christ Who strengthens me.

James 5:11

Indeed we count them blessed who endure. You have heard of the perseverance of Job and seen the end intended by the Lord—that the Lord is very compassionate and merciful.

1 Peter 5:6–7

Therefore humble yourselves under the mighty hand of God, that He may exalt you in due time, casting all your care upon Him, for He cares for you.

1 John 1:9

If we confess our sins, He is faithful and just to forgive us *our* sins and to cleanse us from all unrighteousness.

For Richer or Poorer

Psalm 4:1

Answer me when I call, O God of my righteousness! You have relieved me in my distress; be gracious to me and hear my prayer. (NASB)

Psalm 23:1

The Lord is my shepherd, I lack nothing. (NIV)

Psalm 34:10

The young lions lack and suffer hunger; but those who seek the Lord shall not lack any good thing.

Psalm 37:4

Delight yourself also in the Lord, and He shall give you the desires of your heart.

Psalm 37:25–26

I have been young, and now am old; yet I have not seen the righteous forsaken, nor his descendants begging bread. He is ever merciful, and lends, and His descendants are blessed.

Proverbs 3:5–6

Trust in the Lord with all your heart, and lean not on your own understanding; in all your ways acknowledge Him, and He shall direct your paths.

Proverbs 3:9–10

Honor the Lord with your possessions, and with the firstfruits of all your increase; so your barns will be filled with plenty, and your vats will overflow with new wine.

Proverbs 19:14

Houses and riches are an inheritance from fathers, but a prudent wife is from the Lord.

Proverbs 19:21

Many are the plans in a person's heart, but it is the Lord's purpose that prevails. (NIV)

Proverbs 22:7

The rich rules over the poor, and the borrower becomes the lender's slave. (NASB)

Isaiah 43:19–19

Do not remember the former things, nor consider the things of old. Behold, I will do a new thing, and rivers in the desert.

Jeremiah 29:11

For I know the plans I have for you," declares the Lord, "plans to prosper you and not to harm you, plans to give you hope and a future. (NIV)

Malachi 3:10

"Bring the whole tithe into the storehouse, so that there may be food in My house, and test Me now in this," says the Lord of hosts, "if I will not open for you the windows of heaven and pour out for you a blessing until it overflows." (NASB)

Matthew 6:9–13

Our Father in heaven, hallowed be Your name. Your kingdom come. Your will be done on earth as it is in heaven. Give us this day our daily bread. And forgive us our debts, as we forgive our debtors. And do not lead us into temptation, but deliver us from the evil one. For Yours is the kingdom and the power and the glory forever.

Matthew 6:26–31

Look at the birds of the air, for they neither sow nor reap nor gather into barns; yet your heavenly Father feeds them. Are you not of more value than they? Which of you by worrying can add one cubit to his stature? So why do you worry about clothing? Consider the lilies of the field, how they grow: they neither toil nor spin; and yet I say to you that even Solomon in all his glory was not arrayed like one of these. Now if God so clothes the grass of the field, which today is, and tomorrow is thrown into the oven, will He not much more clothe you, O you of little faith? Therefore do not worry, saying, "What shall we eat?" or "What shall we drink?" or "What shall we wear?"

Matthew 6:33–34

But seek first the kingdom of God and His righteousness, and all these things shall be added to you. Therefore do not worry about tomorrow, for tomorrow will worry about its own things. Sufficient for the day is its own trouble.

Matthew 7:7

Ask, and it will be given to you; seek, and you will find; knock, and it will be opened to you.

Luke 6:38

Give, and it will be given to you. They will pour into your lap a good measure—pressed down, shaken together, and running over. For by your standard of measure it will be measured to you in return. (NSAB)

Luke 14:28

If one of you wanted to build a large building, you would sit down first and think of how much money it would take to build it. You would see if you had enough money to finish it, or when the base of the building is finished, you might see that you do not have enough money to finish it. Then all who would see it would make fun of you. (NIV)

Luke 16:11

So if you have not been trustworthy in handling worldly wealth, who will trust you with true riches? (NIV)

John 15:12

This is My commandment, that you love one another as I have loved you.

John 16:33

These things I have spoken to you, that in Me you may have peace. In the world you will have tribulation; but be of good cheer, I have overcome the world.

Romans 8:28

And we know that all things work together for good to those who love God, to those who are called according to His purpose.

2 Corinthians 9:10–11

Now may He who supplies seed to the sower, and bread for food, supply and multiply the seed you have sown and increase the fruits of your righteousness, while you are enriched in everything for all liberality, which causes thanksgiving through us to God.

Philippians 4:6–8

Be anxious for nothing, but in everything by prayer and supplication, with thanksgiving, let your requests be made known to God; and the peace of God, which surpasses all understanding, will guard your hearts and minds through Christ Jesus. Finally, brethren, whatever things are true, whatever things are noble, whatever things are just, whatever things are pure, whatever things are lovely, whatever things are of good report, if there is any virtue and if there is anything praiseworthy—meditate on these things.

Philippians 4:12

I know how to get along with humble means, and I also know how to live in prosperity; in any and every circumstance I have learned the secret of being filled and going hungry, both of having abundance and suffering need. (NASB)

Philippians 4:19

And my God shall supply all your need according to His riches in glory by Christ Jesus.

2 Timothy 2:23

But avoid foolish and ignorant disputes, knowing that they generate strife.

Hebrews 13:5–6

Keep your lives free from the love of money and be content with what you have, because God has said, "Never will I leave you; never will I forsake you." So we say with confidence, "The Lord is my helper; I will not be afraid. What can mere mortals do to me?" (NIV)

1 John 2:15–17

Do not love the world nor the things in the world. If anyone loves the world, the love of the Father is not in him. For all that is in the world, the lust of the flesh and the lust of the eyes and the boastful pride of life, is not from the Father, but is from the world. The world is passing away, and *also* its lusts; but the one who does the will of God lives forever. (NASB)

1 John 4:7–8

Beloved, let us love one another, for love is of God; and everyone who loves is born of God and knows God. He who does not love does not know God, for God is love.

In Sickness and in Health

Psalm 35:13

But as for me, when they were sick, my clothing *was* sackcloth; I humbled myself with fasting; and my prayer would return to my own heart.

Psalm 41:3

The Lord will strengthen him on his bed of illness; you will sustain him on his sickbed.

Psalm 112:4

Unto the upright there arises light in the darkness; He is gracious, and full of compassion, and righteous.

Proverbs 17:22

A merry heart does good, like medicine, but a broken spirit dries the bones.

Isaiah 30:18

Therefore the Lord will wait, that He may be gracious to you; and therefore He will be exalted, that He may have mercy on you. For the Lord *is* a God of justice; blessed are all those who wait for Him.

Isaiah 40:29–30

He gives strength to the weary and increases the power of the weak. Even youths grow tired and weary, and young men stumble and fall; but those who hope in the Lord will renew their strength. They will soar on wings like eagles; they will run and not grow weary, they will walk and not be faint. (NIV)

Jeremiah 17:14

Heal me, O Lord, and I shall be healed; save me, and I shall be saved, for You are my praise.

Jeremiah 32:27

Behold, I am the Lord, the God of all flesh. Is there anything too hard for Me?

Hosea 6:1

Come, and let us return to the Lord; for He has torn, but He will heal us; He has stricken, but He will bind us up.

Matthew 4:23

And Jesus went about all Galilee, teaching in their synagogues, preaching the gospel of the kingdom, and healing all kinds of sickness and all kinds of disease among the people.

Matthew 7:12

Therefore, whatever you want men to do to you, do also to them, for this is the law and the prophets.

Matthew 18:33

Should you not also have had compassion on your fellow servant, just as I had pity on you?

Matthew 10:1

Jesus summoned His twelve disciples and gave them authority over unclean spirits, to cast them out, and to heal every kind of disease and every kind of sickness. (NASB)

Luke 9:1

Then He (Jesus) called His twelve disciples together and gave them power and authority over all demons, and to cure diseases.

Luke 10:9

Heal the sick who are there and tell them, "The kingdom of God has come near to you."(NIV)

Luke 22:27

For who *is* greater, he who sits at the table, or he who serves? Is it not he who sits at the table? Yet I am among you as the One Who serves.

John 14:1

Let not your heart be troubled; you believe in God, believe also in Me.

Romans 5:3–4

And not only *that,* but we also glory in tribulations, knowing that tribulation produces perseverance; and perseverance, character; and character hope.

Romans 8:18

I consider that our present sufferings are not worth comparing with the glory that will be revealed in us.

Romans 12:10–13

Be kindly affectionate to one another with brotherly love, in honor giving preference to one another; not lagging in diligence, fervent in spirit, serving the Lord; rejoicing in hope, patient in tribulation, continuing steadfastly in prayer; distributing to the needs of the saints, given to hospitality.

1 Corinthians 13:3

And though I bestow all my goods to feed the poor, and though I give my body to be burned, but have not love, it profits me nothing.

2 Corinthians 1:3–5

Blessed be the God and Father of our Lord Jesus Christ, the Father of mercies and God of all comfort, who comforts us in all our tribulation, that we may be able to comfort those who are in any trouble, with the comfort with which we ourselves are comforted by God. For as the sufferings of Christ abound in us, so our consolation also abounds through Christ.

2 Corinthians 4:17

For our light affliction, which is but for a moment, is working for us a far more exceeding and eternal weight of glory,

Galatians 6:2

Carry each other's burdens, and in this way you will fulfill the law of Christ. (NIV)

Galatians 6:9

And let us not grow weary while doing good, for in due season we shall reap if we do not lose heart.

Philippians 2:1–2

Therefore if you have any encouragement from being united with Christ, if any comfort from his love, if any common sharing in the Spirit, if any tenderness and compassion, then make my joy complete by being like-minded, having the same love, being one in spirit and of one mind. (NIV)

Colossians 3:12

Therefore, as God's chosen people, holy and dearly loved, clothe yourselves with Compassion, kindness, humility, gentleness, and patience. (NIV)

1 Thessalonians 5:11

Therefore comfort each other and edify one another, just as you also are doing.

James 5:11

Indeed we count them blessed who endure. You have heard of the perseverance of Job and seen the end intended by the Lord—that the Lord is very compassionate and merciful.

James 5:14

Is anyone among you sick? Let him call for the elders of the church, and let them pray over him, anointing him with oil in the name of the Lord.

1 Peter 2:24

He himself bore our sins in his body on the cross, so that we might die to sins and live for righteousness; by his wounds you have been healed. (NIV)

1 Peter 4:10

As each one has received a gift, minister it to one another, as good stewards of the manifold grace of God.

1 Peter 5:7

Give all your worries and cares to God, for he cares about you. (NLT)

Til Death Do Us Part

Proverbs 3:5–6

Trust in the Lord with all your heart, and lean not on your own understanding; in all your ways acknowledge Him, and He shall direct your paths.

Proverbs 14:1

The wise woman builds her house, but the foolish pulls it down with her hands.

Proverbs 27:17

As iron sharpens iron, so one person sharpens another. (NIV)

Ezekiel 16:8

"When I passed by you again and looked upon you, indeed your time was the time of love; so I spread My wing over you and covered your nakedness. Yes, I swore an oath to you and entered into a covenant with you, and you became Mine," says the Lord God.

Joshua 23:11

Therefore take careful heed to yourselves, that you love the Lord your God.

Matthew 5:4

Blessed are those who mourn, for they shall be comforted.

Matthew 10:17

He who loves father or mother more than Me is not worthy of Me. And he who loves son or daughter more than Me is not worthy of Me.

Mark 10:9

Therefore what God has joined together, let not man separate.

John 15:13

Greater love has no one than this: to lay down one's life for one's friends. (NIV)

Romans 8:28

And we know that all things work together for good to those who love God, to those who are called according to His purpose.

1 Corinthians 7:5

Do not deprive one another except with consent for a time, that you may give yourselves to fasting and prayer; and come together again so that Satan does not tempt you because of your lack of self-control.

1 Corinthians 7:39

A wife is bound by law as long as her husband lives; but if her husband dies, she is at liberty to be married to whom she wishes, only in the Lord.

1 Corinthians 11:8–12

For man does not originate from woman, but woman from man; for indeed man was not created for the woman's sake, but woman for the man's sake. Therefore the woman ought to have a symbol of authority on her head, because of the angels. However, in the Lord, neither is woman independent of man, nor is man independent of woman. For as the woman originates from the man, so also the man has his birth through the woman; and all things originate from God. (NASB)

1 Corinthians 13:4–7

Love suffers long and is kind; love does not envy; love does not parade itself, is not puffed up; does not behave rudely, does not seek its own, is not provoked, thinks no evil; does not rejoice in iniquity, but rejoices in the truth; bears all things, believes all things, hopes all things, endures all things.

2 Corinthians 10:5

We demolish arguments and every pretension that sets itself up against the knowledge of God, and we take captive every thought to make it obedient to Christ.

Galatians 5:22–24

But the fruit of the Spirit is love, joy, peace, longsuffering, kindness, goodness, faithfulness, gentleness, self-control. Against such there is no law. And those who are Christ's have crucified the flesh with its passions and desires.

Ephesians 4:1–3

As a prisoner for the Lord, then, I urge you to live a life worthy of the calling you have received. Be completely humble and gentle; be patient, bearing with one another in love. Make every effort to keep the unity of the Spirit through the bond of peace. (NIV)

Ephesians 4:26

Be angry, and do not sin; do not let the sun go down on your wrath, nor give place to the devil.

Ephesians 5:23

For the husband is head of the wife, as also Christ is head of the church; and He is the Savior of the body.

Ephesians 6:16

Stand therefore, having girded your waist with truth, having put on the breastplate of righteousness, and having shod your feet with the preparation of the gospel of peace; above all, taking the shield of faith with which you will be able to quench all the fiery darts of the wicked one.

Philippians 2:1–2

Therefore if there is any consolation in Christ, if any comfort of love, if any fellowship of the Spirit, if any affection and mercy, fulfill my joy by being like-minded, having the same love, being of one accord, of one mind.

Philippians 2:4
Let each of you look out not only for his own interests, but also for the interests of others.

Philippians 4:8
Finally, brethren, whatever things are true, whatever things *are* noble, whatever things *are* just, whatever things *are* pure, whatever things *are* lovely, whatever things *are* of good report, if *there is* any virtue and if *there is* anything praiseworthy—meditate on these things.

Colossians 1:11
I pray that God's great power will make you strong, and that you will have joy as you wait and do not give up.

Colossians 3:15–19
Let the peace of Christ have power over your hearts. You were chosen as a part of His body. Always be thankful. Let the teaching of Christ and His words keep on living in you. These make your lives rich and full of wisdom. Keep on teaching and helping each other. Sing the Songs of David and the church songs and the songs of heaven with hearts full of thanks to God. Whatever you say or do, do it in the name of the Lord Jesus. Give thanks to God the Father through the Lord Jesus. Wives, obey your husbands. This is what the Lord wants you to do. Husbands, love your wives. Do not hold hard feelings against them.

Colossians 3:23–24
And whatever you do, do it heartily, as to the Lord and not to men, knowing that from the Lord you will receive the reward of the inheritance; for you serve the Lord Christ.

When the Vows Break

Genesis 2:24

Therefore a man shall leave his father and mother and be joined to his wife, and they shall become one flesh.

Numbers 30:2

If a man makes a vow to the Lord, or swears an oath to bind himself by some agreement, he shall not break his word; he shall do according to all that proceeds out of his mouth.

Deuteronomy 4:31

(For the Lord your God *is* a merciful God) He will not forsake you nor destroy you, nor forget the covenant of your fathers which He swore to them.

Deuteronomy 22:19

They shall fine him a hundred shekels of silver and give them to the young woman's father, because this man has given an Israelite virgin a bad name. She shall continue to be his wife; he must not divorce her as long as he lives. (NIV)

Psalm 30:5

For His anger is but for a moment, His favor is for life; weeping may endure for a night, but joy comes in the morning.

Psalm 46:1

God is our refuge and strength, a very present help in trouble.

Psalm 119:50

My comfort in my suffering is this: Your promise preserves my life. (NIV)

Psalm 119:176

I have gone astray like a lost sheep; seek Your servant, for I do not forget Your commandments.

Psalm 145:18–20

The Lord is near to all who call upon Him, to all who call upon Him in truth. He will fulfill the desire of those who fear Him; He also will hear their cry and save them. The Lord preserves all who love Him, but all the wicked He will destroy.

Proverbs 11:29

He who troubles his own house will inherit the wind, and the fool will be servant to the wise of heart.

Proverbs 18:22

He who finds a wife finds a good thing, and obtains favor from the Lord.

Proverbs 27:8

Like a bird that flees its nest is anyone who flees from home.

Isaiah 41:10

Fear not, for I am with you; be not dismayed, for I am your God. I will strengthen you, yes, I will help you, I will uphold you with My righteous right hand.

Isaiah 58:11

The Lord will guide you continually, and satisfy your soul in drought, and strengthen your bones; you shall be like a watered garden, and like a spring of water, whose waters do not fail.

Jeremiah 3:1

"They say, 'If a man divorces his wife, and she goes from him and becomes another man's, may he return to her again?' Would not that land be greatly polluted? But you have played the harlot with many lovers; yet return to Me," says the Lord.

Jeremiah 29:11

For I know the thoughts that I think toward you, says the Lord, thoughts of peace and not of evil, to give you a future and a hope.

Malachi 2:15

But did He not make them one, having a remnant of the Spirit? And why one? He seeks godly offspring. Therefore take heed to your spirit, and let none deal treacherously with the wife of his youth.

Malachi 2:15

"For the Lord God of Israel says that He hates divorce, for it covers one's garment with violence," says the Lord of hosts. "Therefore take heed to your spirit, that you do not deal treacherously."

Matthew 19:8–9

Jesus said to them, "Because of your hard hearts Moses allowed you to divorce your wives. It was not like that from the beginning. I tell you that anyone who divorces his wife, except for sexual immorality, and marries another woman commits adultery." (NIV)

Matthew 5:31–32

"Furthermore it has been said, 'Whoever divorces his wife, let him give her a certificate of divorce.' But I say to you that whoever divorces his wife for any reason except sexual immorality causes her to commit adultery; and whoever marries a woman who is divorced commits adultery.

Matthew 12:25

But Jesus knew their thoughts, and said to them: "Every kingdom divided against itself is brought to desolation, and every city or house divided against itself will not stand."

Mark 10:9

Therefore what God has joined together, let not man separate.

Mark 10:11–12

Whoever divorces his wife and marries another commits adultery against her. And if a woman divorces her husband and marries another, she commits adultery.

Romans 8:38–39

For I am persuaded that neither death nor life, nor angels nor principalities nor powers, nor things present nor things to come, nor height nor depth, nor any other created thing, shall be able to separate us from the love of God which is in Christ Jesus our Lord.

1 Corinthians 7:10–11

Now to the married I command, yet not I but the Lord: A wife is not to depart from her husband. But even if she does depart, let her remain unmarried or be reconciled to her husband. And a husband is not to divorce his wife.

1 Corinthians 7:12–13

To the rest I say this (I, not the Lord): If any brother has a wife who is not a believer and she is willing to live with him, he must not divorce her. And if a woman has a husband who is not a believer and he is willing to live with her, she must not divorce him. (NIV)

1 Corinthians 7:15

But if the unbeliever leaves, let it be so. The brother or the sister is not bound in such circumstances; God has called us to live in peace. (NIV)

1 Corinthians 7:39; Romans 7:2

A wife is bound by law as long as her husband lives; but if her husband dies, she is at liberty to be married to whom she wishes, only in the Lord.

1 Timothy 5:8

But if anyone does not provide for his own, and especially for those of his household, he has denied the faith and is worse than an unbeliever.

Hebrews 13:4

Marriage *is* honorable among all, and the bed undefiled; but fornicators and adulterers God will judge.

James 5:13

Is anyone among you suffering? Let him pray. Is anyone cheerful? Let him sing psalms.

1 Peter 1:3–5

Blessed be the God and Father of our Lord Jesus Christ, who according to His abundant mercy has begotten us again to a living hope through the resurrection of Jesus Christ from the dead, to an inheritance incorruptible and undefiled and that does not fade away, reserved in heaven for you, who are kept by the power of God through faith for salvation ready to be revealed in the last time.

1 Peter 1:6–7

In this you greatly rejoice, though now for a little while, if need be, you have been grieved by various trials, that the genuineness of your faith, being much more precious than gold that perishes, though it is tested by fire, may be found to praise, honor, and glory at the revelation of Jesus Christ.

1 John 4:16

And we have known and believed the love that God has for us. God is love, and he who abides in love abides in God, and God in him.

Revelation 21:3–4

And I heard a loud voice from the throne saying, "Look! God's dwelling place is now among the people, and he will dwell with them. They will be his people, and God himself will be with them and be their God. He will wipe every tear from their eyes. There will be no more death' or mourning or crying or pain, for the old order of things has passed away."

Forgiveness

Psalm 51:10–12

Create in me a clean heart, O God, and renew a steadfast spirit within me. Do not cast me away from Your presence, and do not take Your Holy Spirit from me. Restore to me the joy of Your salvation, and uphold me *by Your* generous Spirit.

Psalm 91:1–2

He who dwells in the secret place of the Most High shall abide under the shadow of the Almighty. I will say of the Lord, "He is my refuge and my fortress; my God, in Him I will trust."

Psalm 103:10–14

He has not dealt with us according to our sins, nor punished us according to our iniquities. For as the heavens are high above the earth, so great is His mercy toward those who fear Him; as far as the east is from the west, so far has He removed our transgressions from us. As a father pities his children, so the Lord pities those who fear Him. For He knows our frame; He remembers that we are dust.

Psalm 119:1–3

Blessed are those whose ways are blameless, who walk according to the law of the Lord. Blessed are those who keep his statutes and seek him with all their heart—they do no wrong but follow his ways. (NIV)

Proverbs 3:5–6

Trust in the Lord with all your heart, and lean not on your own understanding; in all your ways acknowledge Him, and He shall direct your paths.

Proverbs 10:12

Hatred stirs up strife, but love covers all sins.

Proverbs 20:22

Do not say, "I'll pay you back for this wrong!" Wait for the Lord, and he will avenge you. (NIV)

Isaiah 43:25–26

I, even I, am He who blots out your transgressions for My own sake; and I will not remember your sins. Put Me in remembrance; let us contend together; state your case, that you may be acquitted.

Isaiah 53:5

But He was wounded for our transgressions, He was bruised for our iniquities; the chastisement for our peace was upon Him, and by His stripes we are healed.

Matthew 5:22

But I tell you that anyone who is angry with a brother or sister will be subject to judgment. Again, anyone who says to a brother or sister, "Raca," is answerable to the court. And anyone who says, "You fool!" will be in danger of the fire of hell. (NIV)

Matthew 5:44

But I tell you, love your enemies and pray for those who persecute you, that you may be children of your Father in heaven. He causes his sun to rise on the evil and the good, and sends rain on the righteous and the unrighteous. (NIV)

Matthew 6:12

And forgive us our debts, as we forgive our debtors.

Matthew 6:14

For if you forgive men their trespasses, your heavenly Father will also forgive you. But if you do not forgive men their trespasses, neither will your Father forgive your trespasses.

Matthew 7:2

For in the same way you judge others, you will be judged, and with the measure you use, it will be measured to you.

Matthew 11:28–30

Come to Me, all you who labor and are heavy laden, and I will give you rest. Take My yoke upon you and learn from Me, for I am gentle and lowly in heart, and you will find rest for your souls. For My yoke is easy and My burden is light.

Matthew 18:21–22

Then Peter came to Him and said, "Lord, how often shall my brother sin against me, and I forgive him? Up to seven times?" Jesus said to him, "I do not say to you, up to seven times, but up to seventy times seven."

Mark 11:25

And whenever you stand praying, if you have anything against anyone, forgive him, that your Father in heaven may also forgive you your trespasses.

Luke 6:27

But I say to you who hear: Love your enemies, do good to those who hate you.

Romans 12:19

Never take your own revenge, beloved, but leave room for the wrath of God, for it is written, "Vengeance is mine; I will repay" says the Lord. (NASB)

2 Corinthians 2:5–8

But if anyone has caused grief, he has not grieved me, but all of you to some extent—not to be too severe. This punishment which was inflicted by the majority is sufficient for such a man, so that, on the contrary, you ought rather to forgive and comfort him, lest perhaps such a one be swallowed up with too much sorrow. Therefore I urge you to reaffirm your love to him.

Ephesians 4:26

"In your anger do not sin": Do not let the sun go down while you are still angry, and do not give the devil a foothold. (NIV)

Ephesians 4:31–32

Let all bitterness, wrath, anger, clamor, and evil speaking be put away from you, with all malice. And be kind to one another, tenderhearted, forgiving one another, even as God in Christ forgave you.

1 Thessalonians 5:15

See that no one renders evil for evil to anyone, but always pursue what is good both for yourselves and for all.

Hebrews 12:1–2

Therefore we also, since we are surrounded by so great a cloud of witnesses, let us lay aside every weight, and the sin which so easily ensnares us, and let us run with endurance the race that is set before us, looking unto Jesus, the author and finisher of our faith, who for the joy that was set before Him endured the cross, despising the shame, and has sat down at the right hand of the throne of God.

The Last Word

So, as God's own chosen people, who are holy (set apart, sanctified for His purpose) and well-beloved (by God Himself), put on a heart of compassion, kindness, humility, gentleness, and patience (which has the power to endure whatever injustice or unpleasantness comes, with good temper); bearing graciously with one another, and willingly forgiving each other if one has a cause for complaint against another; just as the Lord has forgiven you, so should you forgive. Beyond all these things put on and wrap yourselves in (unselfish) love, which is the perfect bond of unity (for everything is bound together in agreement when each one seeks the best for others). Let the peace of Christ (the inner calm of one who walks daily with Him) be the controlling factor in your hearts (deciding and settling questions that arise). To this peace indeed you were called as members in one body (of believers). And be thankful (to God always). Let the (spoken) word of Christ have its home within you (dwelling in your heart and mind—permeating every aspect of your being) as you teach (spiritual things) and admonish and train one another with all wisdom, singing psalms and hymns and spiritual songs with thankfulness in your hearts to God. Whatever you do (no matter what it is) in word or deed, do everything in the name of the Lord Jesus (and in dependence on Him), giving thanks to God the Father through Him. (Colossians 3:12–25 AMP)

References

Byron, G. Gordon, Lord. 1994. *Byron*. Everyman's Library Pocket Poets Series. New York, London, Toronto: Alfred A. Knopf.

Cary, Phoebe. "Phoebe Cary Quotes." AZ Quotes. http://www.azquotes.com/quote/1159925. (accessed June 23, 2017).

Center for Arizona Policy. 2014. "Marriage & Family; Harms of Divorce." January. http://azpolicypages.com/wp-content/uploads/2013/12/Marriage-Family_HarmsofDivorce.pdf. (accessed July 6, 2017).

Chapman, Gary. 1995. *The Five Love Languages*. Chicago, Illinois: Northfield Publishing.

Copen, Casey E., Kimberly Daniels, Ph.D., and William E. Mosher, Ph.D. "First Premarital Cohabitation in the United States: 2006–-2010 National Survey of Family Growth." Centers for Disease Control and Prevention. National Health Statistics Report. April 4. https://www.cdc.gov/nchs/data/nhsr/nhsr064.pdf (accessed January 27, 2017).

———. "Sexual Risk Behaviors: HIV, STD, & Teen Pregnancy Prevention." October 21, 2017. http://www.cdc.gov/healthyyouth/sexualbehaviors/index.htm (accessed March 2, 2017).

Cowman, Charles E., Mrs. 1996. *Streams in the Desert*. Grand Rapids, Michigan: Zondervan Publishing House.

Curtiz, Michael, director. 1945. Mildred Pierce. Warner Brothers.

Dorsett, Lyle W. 1996. *The Essential C. S. Lewis.* New York, New York: Touchstone.

Drew, Jeffrey, Sonya Britt, and Sandra Huston. 2012. "Examining the Relationship Between Financial Issues and Divorce." The National Council on Family Relations. September 4. http://onlinelibrary.wiley.com/doi/10.1111/j.1741-37 29.2012.00715.x/abstract. (accessed March 2, 2017).

Eggerichs, Emerson, Dr. 2004. *Love & Respect.* Nashville, Tennessee: Thomas Nelson, Inc.

Freeman, James M. 1998. *The New Manners & Customs of the Bible.* Alachua, Florida: Bridge–Logos.

Funk, Charles Earle. 1985. *A Hog on Ice: & Other Curious Expressions.* New York, New York: Harper & Row Publishers, Inc.

Gower, Ralph. 1987. *The New Manners & Customs of Bible Times.* Chicago, Illinois: Moody Press

Harley, Willard F., Jr. 2003. *His Needs, Her Needs.* Grand Rapids, Michigan: Revell.

Hunter, Charles, and Frances. 2008. *Laugh Yourself Happy.* Lake Mary, Florida: Christian Life.

Janssen, Al. 2001. *The Marriage Masterpiece.* Wheaton, Illinois: Tyndale House Publishers.

Krueger, William Kent. 2013. *Ordinary Grace.* New York, New York: Atria.

Lewis, C. S. 1996. The Essential C. S. Lewis. New York, New York: Touchstone.

———. 2012. *The Four Loves.* New York, New York: Mariner Books, Houghton Mifflin Harcourt Publishing.

Miller, Kathy Collard, and D. Larry Miller. 2002. *What's in the Bible for Couples.* Lancaster, Pennsylvania: Starburst Publishers.

National Academy of Sciences. 2013. "Marital Satisfaction and Break-Ups Differ Across On-Line and Off-Line Meeting Venues." Proceedings of the National Academy of Sciences of the United States of America (PNAS). May 1. http://www.pnas.org/content/110/25/10135.full (accessed March 27, 2017).

Pew Research Center. 2017. "Marriage." Society and Demographics. http//www.pewresearch.org/data-trend/society-and-demographic

Quigley, Mary. 2017. "Popping the Question: Who Pays?" AARP Bulletin 58, 5: 22.

Ridolfi, Brian. 2005. *"What Does the Bible Say About…: The Ultimate Bible Answer Book"* Chattanooga, Tennessee: AMG Publishers.

Seamands, David A. 1992. Healing for Damaged Emotions. Wheaton, Illinois: Victor Books.

———. 1995. *Healing of Memories*. Carmel, New York: Guideposts.

Shapiro, Fred R. 2006. *The Yale Book of Quotations*. New Haven, Connecticut, London, England: Yale University Press.

Swindoll, Chuck. 2015. "Looking Ahead to Things That Last, Part 1." Insight for Living. National Public Radio (NPR). November 12.

United States Wedding Statistics. "Cost of Wedding." United States Wedding Statistics. The Wedding Report, Inc. http://www.costofwedding.com. (accessed June 28, 2017).

Wildstein, Jeffrey. 2015. Idiot's Guide: *Judaism*. New York, New York: Penguin Random House LLC.

Young, Ed. 1997. *Pure Sex*. Sisters, Oregon: Multnomah Publishing, Inc.

www.ingramcontent.com/pod-product-compliance
Lightning Source LLC
LaVergne TN
LVHW011221080426
835509LV00005B/243